SELL IT!
THERE'S A JOB
FOR EVERYONE

Earn while you learn! Anyone can do it.

By

William S. Crenshaw

DEDICATION

I dedicate this book to those people who dream the dreams and are willing to pay the price to make them come true.

A great philosopher once said:
"Whatever you can do, or think you can, begin it;
Boldness has genius, power and magic in it."

- Johann Wolfgang von Goethe -
1749 – 1832

PREFACE

After spending almost 50 years in sales, and building a life most people just dream about, I realize it's time to pay-it-forward, and help others find their ultimate careers.

During the last ten years, leading corporations have approached me with tempting offers to become a motivational speaker on their behalf. And colleges in my area have asked me to teach, as well. But that seemed too confining.

Like most other successful people, I tend to be very passionate about the things I believe in, and I've always hated the idea of having to be politically correct when it comes to airing my thoughts and views.

So not to be influenced by outside sources, I decided to write a book to share my knowledge with you through a series of, thought-provoking, real life stories.

Since sales has been my life, and salespeople my best friends, I have the ultimate respect for them and the careers they've chosen. Many of them are highly educated, while others only finished high school. Then there are those who dropped out of school at an early age to help support their families. But they all have certain things in common... among them are faith, courage, self-motivation and determination, which inevitably led to their success.

In my world, you don't need a college degree to become a top wage earner, or a respected member of society. However, you must continually strive to acquire more knowledge, because knowledge is power in sales.

By passing my knowledge on to you, I hope you will learn how to turn your ambition into commission. In sales, there truly is a job for everyone and you can earn while you learn. Remember, every time someone says yes, its money in your pocket.

TABLE OF CONTENTS

CHAPTER 1
THE GREATEST JOB IN THE WORLD

Discover the power that keeps all businesses running, and you'll find there's a job for everyone!

It's amazing how hard it is to find the perfect job, especially if you're looking in all the wrong places. Many people don't seriously think of sales for a career, but if they understood the driving force behind every business, they might reconsider. Money is the power source that keeps all businesses running and only sales can keep it fueled. Once you understand that, you'll realize there's a career in sales for everyone.

Just for fun, close your eyes and imagine a place where there are jobs for the taking and endless possibilities everywhere you look. I can see it clearly, can you? Once you realize how each business functions, you'll know what to look for. Then open your

1

eyes to the world around you and you'll discover that imaginary place is real ... you are already there!

Whether you are unemployed or dissatisfied with the job you currently have, you should begin by learning about business in general, then look for your new career. After you do, you'll realize there are more job opportunities than you could have ever imagined. They were there all along, hidden in plain-sight.

Since a business can't operate without money, it just stands to reason, that there are more sales positions available than any other. Once you understand basic business principles and learn how to sell, you can choose the field you want to work in and earn a great living doing what you would like to do.

Next, look at the person you've become and then think of the person you would like to be. Are you unemployed, looking for work and hoping someone will give you a job? If you are, you're a needy person, and you can't bargain from a position of weakness. So, start believing in yourself, and show a little confidence.

Instead of telling someone you need a job, learn how to sell yourself and tell them that you are a professional salesperson who has the ability to sell their products and services. Then ask them what commission they are willing to pay you for each sale you close.

Now, you're not a needy person anymore. You are exceptional. You have a vital service to offer. Remember, a successful salesperson is a valuable commodity. They make excellent money for the company they work for and themselves, and they are always in demand. Once you're confident in yourself, and learn how to perform as a topnotch salesperson, the whole world will open up for you.

When I was young I had a chance to earn a little cash by selling things in the city I grew up in, but I never thought of sales as a life-long career. I only pitched odds 'n' ends as a quick fix to make easy money. The idea that sales could change my life forever never crossed my mind.

In the 1950s and '60s, everyone's focus was on how much you could earn if you were a doctor, lawyer, or accountant, and how prestigious those jobs were. My parents wanted me to become a high-paid professional in a specialized field, and they said that could never happen unless I graduated from a top-notch university.

With that in mind, higher education was all we talked about at my house and freedom wasn't part of any job-description.

Later on, however, I would witness first hand, that a degree was no guarantee of landing a good job or keeping it, and that realization confused me for years.

It's strange looking back, during all of my formative years, not one of my teachers or counselors ever suggested a career in sales. Our school curriculum was designed to give us a diversified education built around: reading, writing, arithmetic, social studies, history, art, music, sports, (or physical education), home economics and science. No one ever thought of teaching the art of sales. Nor did they consider how important selling would be if we were to become successful in any of those fields.

In high school, joining the debate team or taking public speaking was as close as you could get to a class in sales. However, even that fell far short from teaching you how to understand the field of sales. And no one talked about finding a job that would offer you the ultimate in freedom. As a matter-of-fact, freedom and success, all rolled-into-one seemed like an absurd idea until I read an article in the Readers Digest about a man named Dean Alfange. This man loved being an American, and more than anything, he cherished his freedom.

To share his views of how he thought we should live our lives, and what it meant to be an American, he wrote An American Creed, and it went something like this:

"In America you do not have to be a common man. It is your right to be uncommon if you can. Seek opportunity, not security. Do not wish to be a kept citizen, humbled and dulled by having the state look after you. Take the calculated risk, to dream and to build, to fail and to succeed. Refuse to trade incentive for charity. Instead, prefer the challenges of life to the guaranteed existence, the thrill of fulfillment to the stale calm of utopia. Do not trade freedom for profit nor your dignity for a handout. Never cower before any master nor bend to any threat. It is your heritage to stand erect, proud and unafraid, to think and act for yourself, enjoy the benefits of your creations and to face the world boldly and say, this I have done. All this is what it means to be an American."

To me, this article said it all. Freedom did not come without risk, and the perfect job did not come with guarantees. But what was the perfect job?

Most high paying occupations were so time-consuming that professionals had little or no time left to enjoy the fruits of their labors. The average professional couldn't drop what they were doing at a moment's notice and take off any time they pleased.

5

So, had they actually found the perfect job, or were they trapped?

Doctors borrowed and spent hundreds of thousands of dollars and devoted many years of their lives to earn a degree, so they could practice medicine, and then they started their lives in debt. Once they ventured out on their own, they were constantly on call, shackled to a hospital or their practice.

Lawyers went through the same scenario only to be kept on a tight leash by the courts and pressing cases.

As for accountants, they were confronted with never ending changes by our governments antiquated tax code system. During tax season, they seemed to spend every waking hour at their office trying to beat the deadline for turning in tax returns. And every year they had to take additional classes to keep up with the new tax laws that were put on the books.

I also watched many family members lose their jobs just as they started thinking of retirement, and that taught me a serious lesson. You don't want to be fooled by the glitter of a flashy corporate position or feel secure because you work for a giant corporation.

The companies my relatives went to work for began by promising them the moon and stars, with benefits such as health care, a retirement account, paid

SELL IT! There's A Job For Everyone

vacations, company cars, credit-cards and a bonus at the end of the year. By painting this rosy picture and suggesting they would review their job performance on a regular basis for salary increases, these giant companies lulled them into a false sense of security making each one feel important. They thought their jobs would last forever, but that turned out to be far from the truth.

It turns out that a major fallacy in most corporate promises is the retirement package or pension plan. In this fantasy, all you have to do is become a company man, or woman, and dedicate yourself to the business until its retirement time, then you'll be taken care of for the rest of your life. When you hear this, you should be thinking it sounds too good to be true! But the warmth of the security blanket they're wrapping around you at the time, and the vision of utopia can cloud your mind and start you daydreaming of a bright future.

What they won't tell you when you're being recruited is the fact that this beautiful dream is often unsustainable, and most corporations have no intention of keeping their word. You see, the promise of a lifetime pension is extremely expensive. It's also easy for them to get out of that obligation, so they won't have to pay you in the end.

7

As you approach retirement age, the corporation you're working for can save a bundle of money by getting you to leave early. Then they can hire another person to take your place for half the pay, or a beginners-salary, and start the process again.

If you refuse to go along with this plan, they can make your job unbearable. If that doesn't get you to take an early retirement they can simply make your job disappear, so what choice will you have?

Another common occurrence that crushes many corporate employees is becoming the victim of a slowdown in the economy. If the economy drops off, you better hope heaven will help you, because the corporations won't. When it comes right down to it, most corporations think of salaried employees as nothing more than dollar signs and high paid executives are often the first people to be let go when a business slows down.

It just stands to reason that everything a company gives, or pays out to its' employees, is part of its overhead. Now the pay-raises you've earned through the years and your impressive job position and entitlements have become a costly problem for the struggling business. To try and save their selves most corporations will immediately cut back on expenses, and you will find yourself out of work and back on the streets.

What's even worse is usually the timing of becoming jobless. Like most things in your life, timing is crucial, and losing your job in the middle of your peak, or prime moneymaking years, can be devastating. This loss of income can never be recuperated.

By this time, I had witnessed something everyone should remember ... corporations promise a lot and give as little as possible. If what they tell you, sounds too good to be true, then it probably isn't true at all. I also realized there are no guarantees. You can't go back and make up for lost time if you make the wrong choice when you choose your career.

These events taught me to think carefully when searching for a job. I needed to find a career that wouldn't stagnate in my 40s and 50s, leaving me with little or no opportunity to expand my earning potential, as I got older. I also needed a position in the work place that would be the least likely to get downsized during a slowing economy.

After considering everything, a career in sales made perfect sense to me. Independent salespeople had to be the freest people on earth, and they controlled their own destinies. They decided whom they would be working with and where they would be

9

working each day. They also did what they pleased when they pleased... their time was their own. Independent salespeople were also some of the highest paid people in the world, generally making as much, if not more, than the yearly income of doctors, lawyers and accountants. There was no cap or limitation placed on what a salesperson could earn. The sky was the limit!

Now my mind was racing. I knew that once I learned how to perform as a top-notch salesperson I would never have to worry about looking for a job again. All I had to do was pick a field, or subject, and go after it. It was my chance to pursue the American dream. From this time on, I did not have to be a common man; it was my right to be uncommon if I can. I was ready to seek opportunity over security, and open-ended wages, called commissions, sounded like the chance of a lifetime. I didn't need what most people called job security or a steady paycheck. That was just a trap sealing your fate.

Most people gave up their freedom, and their dreams, for a guaranteed paycheck and they never got a chance to see how far they could go in life.

As for me, all I wanted and needed was to find a reputable company with a quality product to sell, and my self-motivation and determination would make me a

SELL IT! There's A Job For Everyone

success. I was ready to take the calculated risk to fail and to succeed. Becoming a salesman would truly give me a chance to earn an exceptional living and enjoy my freedom at the same time. This would be the perfect job.

When I first mentioned the idea of becoming a salesman to my parents, they began squirming in their seats. Like most other people, they never stopped to think about the fact that everything in the world had to be sold, or the entire human race would come to a standstill.

As far back as they could remember the average person on the street thought of salespeople as fast talking hustlers or conmen. The first images of a salesman that came to mind for most folks were usually slick politicians on the campaign trail. Or a sleazy guy at a used car lot telling some poor schmuck what a great buy a worthless old clunker was. In their minds-eye, the political pitch was a load of crap, and the car in question was probably being held together by bubble gum and baling wire. That meant whoever listened to their line-of-bull was doomed to pay a high price for being so foolish or gullible. In reality, salespeople came in every different size, shape, and color. Though there were some con artists in the field of sales, the same was true in every profession. Most people in sales were

11

every bit as hardworking and honest as people in any other occupation.

Truly gifted salespeople had become Presidents, Doctors, Lawyers, Architects, Engineers, Inventors, Preachers, Teachers, and some of our most highly respected visionaries. The best-of-the-best in sales were well-read individuals with a gift of gab that could warm your heart and fill your mind with hope, direction, and purpose. If not for some of our most talented salespeople, we never would have had leaders to follow through our darkest hours, or been able to envision the moon mission. As a matter-of-fact, every brilliant idea had to be sold, or it would never have seen the light of day. It took a great salesman to say we're going to land a man on the moon and make you believe it.

Because of talented salespeople, we have been able to wake up the world and open their eyes and minds to new philosophies, products, and a different way of life.

Some of our greatest communicators like Benjamin Franklin, Walt Disney, John F. Kennedy, Ronald Reagan and Martin Luther King Jr. were salesmen at heart, and they brought their visions to reality by pitching their concepts to the world. Thanks to great communicators, or salesmen, if you will, we have been able to bring down walls, unite people, conquer space, change laws for the better and make our dreams come true.

After learning all of this, I was able to say with certainty that *being a salesperson is truly the greatest job in the world.* I also knew that whatever life-long profession I chose to pursue, learning how to become a top-notch salesman would be the key to my success.

When I began chasing my dreams in 1966, my first job was working at a high-end furniture store. This experience was heaven sent when it came to learning the fine art of sales. My hunger for knowledge, artistic ability, and determination soon paid off. Within three years, I was offered a full partnership in a new 16,000 square foot design studio named Key West Designs. It had only taken four years for me to go from working as a laborer, at a paint manufacturing company in Los Angeles, to owning half of the most beautiful furniture store and design studio in Central California. To make things even better, I was debt free. I owed all of my good fortune to sales.

The first ten years of my multifaceted career were spent in retail sales and design. Then I opened an advertising agency in 1975 and spent the next 35 years developing sales campaigns for a wide range of diversified companies.

13

For over three decades, my work has appeared in campaigns throughout the United States and Europe. I have also won awards in International contests including top honors in the Printing Industries of America Competition. Along with that, I have also had the honor of having three pieces of my artwork hang in the White House in Washington, DC, and millions of my posters have sold to collectors worldwide.

My job as a promoter, during this time, has been to elevate any person, place, or thing, above all others of a like nature. Working behind the scenes has been an education in itself.

This experience has given me an up-close and personal look at the unique characteristics that are found in successful salespeople. A few of them are:

1. An exceptional salesperson is self-motivated, confident, and fiercely independent. They do not like taking orders, or having overseer's hovering around them.

2. Most of them believe in the adage lead, follow, or get out of the way.

3. Exceptional earners are well read and constantly crave more knowledge on a wide range of diversified subjects.

4. They love communicating with people, sharing information, and new ideas.

5. The best salespeople manage their time wisely, but they aren't clock-watchers. They don't care if it's 8:00 in the morning or 5:00 in the evening, instead they will work whenever and wherever the opportunity presents itself, and they usually put in more than the average eight-hour workday.

6. Good salespeople are passionate individuals who can't wait to find out everything they can about a product or service and share that knowledge with everyone they meet.

7. Outstanding salespeople have creative minds and are inventive when it comes to figuring out new ways to get the attention of prospective buyers.

8. A talented salesperson loves the game of selling. In most cases, going after a sale is as stimulating as a good game of chess or poker.

9. Every successful salesperson prepares for each encounter with a prospective client, in much the same way they would prepare for

a game. They know that preparation is the key to success.

10. All outstanding salespeople look forward to a lively debate. As a matter-of-fact, most of your top salespeople can take up either side of an issue and defend, sell or promote it with the same fervor because the challenge for a skilled salesperson is selling the idea itself.

11. Good salespeople love to write up a sale. No matter what size, large or small, the mere fact that they have closed a deal is always the ultimate high for them.

12. The best salesperson is not afraid of taking charge of their own lives and embracing freedom. They have learned that saving money and starting their own retirement plan isn't as hard as it sounds. If they need help setting things up in the beginning, there are a lot of professionals specializing in retirement and pension planning, and being personally involved in their own future is always a good thing. The more information they learn along the way the safer their savings will be.

Through the years, I've found being a salesperson definitely has some wonderful advantages. Not only is the pay fantastic after you've gotten in the groove, with your chosen product or service, but the money keeps getting better as you age all the way up to retirement, and sometimes beyond.

In the field of sales, the older you get, the wiser you get, and that's excellent for business. The most important perks of all for a career in sales are job security, escalating pay and personal freedom.

This cannot be said for many occupations. That's why so many sharp individuals have taken their lives, and careers, into their own hands and said, "I don't need you to take care of me. Just give me all of the money I earn and step out of my way... I can take care of myself. Thank you very much!"

As I was writing this story, I came across an article written by Ellen Schultz and Jessica Silver-Greenberg for the Wall Street Journal titled, "The Other Midlife Crisis." This scary scenario is a reality few people are aware of during the moneymaking prime of their lives.

"It seems, according to the most recent information gathered from the Current Population Survey, a joint effort between the Bureau of Labor Statistics and the Census Bureau, shows that income

17

grows at a steady rate for people in their 20s and 30s. No surprise there. But once people hit midlife, the good times are over. The 40s are the peak earning years for most, when the median income for men and women working full-time hovers between $52,000 in their early 40s and about $54,000 in their late 40s. After that, median income barely budges... It's still $54,000 for men and women aged 50 to 54. In other words, there is a 15-year plateau."

"Cost-of-living adjustments are about all they can count on after they enter their 40s, and a lot of people aren't even getting those." It goes on to say that, "Indeed, according to government statistics, the median earnings of men and women who work full-time fall 10% as they move from their peak earning years toward their retirement years. So even if you continue to work, long after you're eligible for Social Security, you can't count on a rise in your earnings."

It's tempting to think this is mainly a problem for lower-wage workers, but it is also a fact of life for higher-income managers and other professionals. The stagnation in salaries has hit all varieties of workers, from executives to middle managers. What's worse, if any worker loses his or her job while, in their 50s, it will be increasingly difficult to find another high-paying job. Statistics revealed, by the National Employment Law

Project, showed that only 14% of the new jobs were found in higher wage industries compared with 49% for lower-wage industries.

While all this doom and gloom paints a sad ending for many hard working individuals, there is a profession that's almost the complete opposite from the statistics shown above... that occupation is sales! In sales, an average man or woman can earn $50,000 to $60,000 a year in their 30s and 40s. And it's quite common for the same people to earn $65,000 to $100,000 a year from age 50 all the way to retirement. I have had men and women age 60, all the way up to 75 years old, outsell every young salesperson with my company, and bring in a regular yearly income in the six-figure range.

The reason for this unique phenomenon is the fact that the average buyer, for almost any product you can think of, seems to be very comfortable making a purchase from a polite, well-spoken mature man or woman and finds their knowledge, attentiveness, and polite manners refreshing. These characteristics can be the key ingredients to landing large sales and collecting giant commission checks.

In the field of sales, young and old people alike control their own destiny. Since they are only paid for the sales they generate, they are not looked upon as a cost or liability for any company. Because every

19

business needs sales to exist, talented salespeople are a company's most valuable allies, and they are treated as such. Most companies today place their greatest hope for not just surviving, but thriving, on the strength of their salespeople. That is why a job in sales offers so much promise.

As a matter-of-fact, an article on the best of the best business careers available, even during a down economy, recently appeared on the Internet, and was also featured on Yahoo Education, under In-Demand.

The article was written by Chris Kyle and stated that if you are now looking for a new career path, despite the recent financially troubled times, business careers are in demand and are well positioned for solid growth opportunities.

And U. S. News & World Report in its "50 best careers" listed #1- Accountant's as their top pick with an average income of $68,960. The #2- occupation was Financial Advisor with an average income of $91,220. #3- was Public Relations Specialist with an average income of $57,830. #4- was a Financial Analyst with an average income of $86,040. #5- was Human Resources Training Specialist with an average income of $57,830. #6- was an Actuary with an average income of $98,640. #7- was a Meeting Planner with an average income of $48,780. **#8- was a Sales**

Manager, with the average earnings of $114,110.
And #9- was a Logistician with the average earnings of
$73,510.

As you can clearly see, the Sales Manager was
the highest paid by far. And the glowing comments
about the jobs potential for employment growth made it
a real eye-catcher for anyone reading the article. This
same article went on to say that due to the importance
of the Sales Manager in any organization, no matter
what size it is, sales managers are less likely to get
downsized than any other position.

The U.S. Department of Labor is also forecasting
a 15% bump in new employment opportunities for sales
managers for many years to come. What's even more
exciting is the fact that this is just one of thousands of
job opportunities available in the field of sales.

These statistics offer proof of how rewarding a
career in sales can be.

William S. Crenshaw

CHAPTER 2

CONSIDERING A CAREER IN SALES?

If you decide to begin a career in the field of sales, one of the first things you should do is think about the selling process, and all the different types of sales jobs there are from which to choose. You should look before you leap.

Remember, every field of endeavor has its salespeople, and companies are always looking for someone new who can talk the talk, and walk the walk. However, the trick to being both successful and happy in your new sales position is making sure you have chosen the right fit for your talent and personality.

The easiest way to begin this process is to pick something you truly like, and study it. Who manufactures the product you dream of selling? How many different qualities of the product are available? And how many different price ranges are there?

23

On the other hand, if you have chosen a service to sell, who offers it? Who can benefit from using it? And what territories will be the most alluring, for both you and the customers.

Does the product or service you have chosen, require any particular education, degree, or license to sell it? Are you thinking about selling these products or services wholesale, to the retail storeowner, or retail to the public, or end user?

After you have thought about all this, but before you make any decisions, it wouldn't hurt to think over the possibility of selling something entirely different from what others might sell.

When it comes to sales, there are literally millions of conceptual items just waiting for a super-salesperson to sell them. These products range from intellectual properties, to some of the worlds most anticipated new inventions. Every one of these treasures will need to be romanced and sold if they will ever find their way into our hearts and minds. What's more, there are millions, if not billions of dollars to be made by the salespeople with the courage, and insight, to take on these challenges.

Now, since I have teased your brain, and stimulated your thought process, it's time for you to write down every item, service, or concept you would be interested in selling. Don't worry about the whys, and why not's at this stage of the game, just get everything you think of down on paper, or on your computer.

Next, go back over your list and reposition each item in order, based upon the amount of excitement you would feel if you could earn a living selling that product or service. Then use all the criteria listed above to determine which one would be best for you. Most important of all don't forget to dream!

Now it is time for you to hit the books, library, or computer, to begin the learning process. Whatever you have picked to sell, you must learn everything you can about it. Remember, reading is the best place to begin. Knowledge is power in sales.

As you study the subject, you have chosen, be honest with yourself. Some products or services sell best in areas you might not enjoy. Would you want to build a life in that region, or part of the world? If you wouldn't, pass on it, and keep looking. Don't forget every time you move to a new city you essentially have to start over from scratch. That will take a toll on your overall lifetime earnings.

It's also not wise to begin your career by selling something that you don't believe in, or pitching a product or service that you don't personally like. This

25

always ends up in disaster. Do not be easily swayed when making a decision about your job or future. You will become what you settle for.

As you think things through, it will soon become clear whether you have found your niche and chosen the right subject to sell.

When choosing a job, be picky, and you will be happy!

In one of Steve Jobs last commencement speeches, he told the graduating class, "Don't let the noise of others opinions drown out your inner voice. And most important have the courage to follow your heart and intuition, they somehow know what you truly want to become. Everything else is secondary."

If one of the key ingredients for your dream-job involves getting dressed up every day and surrounding yourself with rooms full of gorgeous things, retail sales will put you right where you want to be. Many of the most beautiful architectural environments in the world have been designed and built to offer the most discriminating retail storeowners, their salespeople, and clientele those exact accommodations.

However, if dressing up for work is not your style, there are more casual retail sales outlets to choose from than you can imagine. It's essential that the store you pick to work in, feels comfortable because you'll be spending a lot of time there.

After considering all this, if you think you might feel bored, or trapped, having to work at the same location every day, you might want to try a job in outside sales.

There are salespeople who love the stability inside retail sales brings to their lives, but others have a certain wonder-lust and crave the great outdoors. To them, every new doorway represents the thrill of discovering a new customer, and the opportunity to make a large sale. Outside salespeople love to travel, and they find it hard to sit inside a retail store, waiting for customers to arrive. When business is slow, they would rather go out and stir things up in the streets.

If you connect more with this type of individual, outside sales might be the perfect match for your free-spirited personality.

Outside salespeople are vital in the manufacturing, transportation, distribution, and service industries, and there are thousands of jobs from which to choose.

Every storefront, in every city throughout the world, has goods and merchandise that was sold to them by outside salespeople. These salespeople represent some of the worlds leading manufactures,

27

importers and exporters, and that's just a tiny sampling of what's available to sell.

Like the French say, "Vive la difference." In sales, there truly is a job for everyone. It doesn't matter what environment you would like to work in, or where your interests lie.

Both retail and outside salespeople have the ability to earn the same fantastic incomes, so earning potential should not enter into the equation when making this choice. This decision should only be based on where you will be the happiest!

Once you find the perfect fit for your sales personality, the rest of your life will be filled with challenges, excitement, and rewards beyond your wildest dreams, just as it has been for me.

Now, if you have chosen the subject you would like to dive into, and think you know where you would like to pursue your new career in sales; there are a number of jobs ahead of you.

First, you want to learn as much as possible about the city you are considering. Unless you already live there, the best way to do that is to subscribe to the local newspaper. By reading the local newspaper, on a regular basis, you will be able to get a feeling as to what the city is like. Everything, from its editorials to its advertising will give you a well-rounded picture of what the city is all about, and what it has to offer.

You should be especially interested in what the weather conditions are year round, and what type of housing is available. Next, discover what is going on in the business community, and find out what variety of entertainment there is. What is the current population and how stable is the city's current financial condition? What is the crime rate? What kinds of retail stores are located in the city? Is the area best known for buying and selling goods? Or has it established itself as a manufacturing hub? Last, but not least, you will want to know how many opportunities for employment are currently listed for the sales field you have chosen?

You should also be aware of one other thing. There are usually twice as many job opportunities in every field, than there are postings in the help wanted ads. You just have to learn how to go out and find them.

Next, you should obtain a local phone book, and look through the yellow page listings for a broader view of what the city and outlining areas have to offer. After you look through the phone book, and study the newspapers, create a strategy for working your way into the city you have chosen. Then review the list and

29

determine how, and when, you will be able to complete everything you have laid out.

The most successful salespeople are well-organized, hardworking individuals who stay focused and on schedule. You must think of this exercise as a job you were hired to do, so do not become sidetracked and do not procrastinate!

Once you've gained as much book knowledge on your chosen subject as possible, it's time to start going out on field trips where you will discover a whole new prospective about your dream job, up-close-and-personal. This will give you a chance to find out what is expected of someone who sells the type of product or service you are considering.

Field trips are fun, and they can be highly productive. When you begin venturing out, do not be shy. Ask many questions. You will be surprised how helpful people are when you ask them questions about something they are familiar with, especially if they do it for a living. A proud individual can be a wealth of information, and most people love to brag about their jobs. Next, learn how they dress for work and what their standard hours are. Then find out what distances they travel to perform their duties, etc.

Hopefully by now you will have a little knowledge about the basic product, or service, you have decided to sell. Since you are prepared, you can use that insight to work your way into one-on-one conversations with the people you meet during these outings.

Back during my lean years, I had a Volkswagen. It was cheap on gas, so a field trip was a terrific opportunity to get away from reality. I just packed a sandwich, plotted a course, and away I went, but I always had an agenda.

What I made sure to remember was the fact that I was going on each trip with a purpose in mind. So, in order to stay focused I thought ahead about what I hoped to accomplish on every journey and made a list.

Upon my return home, I sat down and noted what took place, and what I would do differently on my next outing. My main goal, for every field trip, was to learn everything about my prospective new career. I also wanted to see, and be seen. This strategy soon paid off.

By asking questions, I found out that a few sales positions take specialized training and a college degree, but the vast majority of sales jobs can be learned at home, or on the streets. What makes this approach even better is the fact that you can earn while you learn.

Unless you want to sell chemicals, pesticides, or possibly become a nuclear physicist, doctor, lawyer or accountant, no one cares whether you have a college degree. All they care about is whether you have the ability to sell their products or services. If you can, they will be more than willing to give you a cut of the profits. This compensation is called a commission. Remember, every company needs a steady flow of sales to stay alive, and if you can sell their goods, you will be their hero.

All I have is a high school education, and yet I have made a fortune in three separate fields through sales.

By this time, the field trips you have been taking should make you feel a lot more knowledgeable about the subject you've chosen. And the closer you actually get to those working situations, the more comfortable you will become.

During this period, you will want to look for job openings, and learn how to get your foot in the door. This will be your first chance to make a sale, and the first thing you must sell is yourself.

Creating opportunities, and landing your first job, takes a competitive spirit, which anyone can develop. Whether your current personality is that of a soft-spoken individual, or a high-strung player, games like: Chess; Poker; Monopoly; Risk; The Game of Life; and others, are perfect for honing your skills. You can also

SELL IT! There's A Job For Everyone

play each of these free games with family members, or friends.

When you play these games, it is essential for you to start thinking of every move as a strategy you might use in the field, and be willing to take a risk. After that, learn how and when it makes sense to invest in your hand, to better your position. Then learn how to lead your opponent and play a bluff when the time is right.

Next, you need to realize the fact that almost every situation you come across in life can be reduced to a mathematical equation. The simplest form of this is flipping a coin, heads or tails. No matter how you look at it, the coin toss gives you a 50-50 chance to win, so learn how to play the percentages and put the odds in your favor.

These challenging games will bring out the best qualities in you, and help fine-tune that, "take a chance" attitude you need to become successful. Once you have mastered that state of mind, it will pay you huge dividends when it comes to being brave enough to ask for, and land, the job of your dreams.

When you become knowledgeable, confident, and have your game face on, it will be time for you to start looking at the world around you with a different attitude. Now you won't be confused by your surroundings. You will clearly see what's in front of you, and everything you come in contact with will make you daydream about the possibility of another sales opportunity.

After you make a personal commitment to this journey, your life will change for the better. The future will have a lot more to offer, and you will feel stronger and more confident in yourself. But others close to you might seem to be confused by the course you've taken.

The whole concept of making your way through life with no guarantee, or safety net, is viewed by some people as a foolhardy thing to do. Because of that consensus, only those who understand will realize you have a plan! Now you are the captain of your destiny and the master of your soul.

When I first ventured out on my own, I found a job that paid an hourly wage. Although the job gave me security, the work I performed left me empty inside. Every morning, when I got up and sat down at the breakfast table, I knew what was expected of me. I was supposed to go to work, do my job, and collect my pay. But this occupation left me nothing to dream of and little hope for the future. No matter how hard I worked, the only way I could earn extra money was to put in overtime, or hope for a pay raise someday.

But when I landed my first sales position, I couldn't wait to get out of the house in the morning. I remember saying, "I'm off to make my fortune," and I meant it!

From that time on, every day has been filled with dreams of what incredible things I could accomplish and the adventures that are in store for me.

I believe these three words best describe a job in sales: hope, dreams and freedom. But remember, with freedom, comes responsibility.

Once you choose this lifestyle, it will be up to you to map out your own strategies. You will also be free to control your own economic destiny. This can be extremely intoxicating, to say the least. The problem is, most people who become wealthy before they are prepared for it, are broke soon after.

It's sad to say, but when it comes to making and spending money, it's usually easy come, easy go, unless you learn how to manage your income wisely.

When you worked for an hourly wage and your monthly paychecks never varied, it wasn't hard to figure out a budget and stay within it. You just listed your rent, average utilities, essential household needs, possibly a car payment and insurance, and your job was done. By the time you got that far, you had run out of money, so you couldn't mess things up. And, if you were smart, you stayed out of stores so as not to temp yourself with things you couldn't afford to purchase.

35

Another thought that kept your spending in line was the chance of losing your job if the economy slowed down. Fear of losing your job alone, kept your mind from running wild with fantasies of lavish spending sprees. However, once you enter the field of sales, it's possible to make more money than you could have ever imagined. This instant cash flow is a temptation that can wreak havoc on an unprepared newbie in sales, so it's imperative that you learn how to budget and plan for the future.

The single biggest threat of all, to the career of a new salesperson, is the bottomless pit known as… **The Time Payment Plan!**

Here, for the sake of instant gratification, many a newbie has sold their soul, and traded in their freedom for something they could have lived without. Now, after this new salesperson signed their name on the dotted line, they became slaves to the monthly time payment plan.

With that one poor decision, they gave up their chance to earn unlimited income, and traded it in for an eight-to-five job just to make the strokes and keep the creditors off their backs. In most cases that marked the end of their chance to know how far they could have gone in life, and how much they could have earned.

Professional salespeople love their freedom and would never give it up, or sell it, for something shinny in a store window.

As a newcomer, to sales, you have to realize that you must learn how to take charge of your spending habits and use your commission checks differently than salaried individuals who live payday to payday on their hourly, or monthly fixed paychecks.

Because you have to prepare for success, it will be imperative that you get your affairs in order.

First, you should create a strategy to get all of your current bills like credit cards, and any other time payment plans you have, paid off as soon as possible. Next, you must learn to think of how successful you will become if you can keep your wants in check while you take care of your needs. Freedom is being debt free!

Salespeople who learn patience wind up having it all, and the ones that want everything now end up broke.

In this new position, it's quite common to make a large sale shortly after you start your job and wind up with a commission check equal to half a year's income. The following month, however, you might hit a dry spell when nothing seems to close. Then you will find yourself to be hurting if you squandered your enormous paycheck.

Most seasoned professionals prepare a written list, or budget, of what they intend to spend, month to month, and prioritize it. Next they give themselves a monthly allowance and only spend what's on that list. Anything left over goes in the bank. They know from experience how important a savings account will be.

Remember, you want to think of yourself like a business and build up your savings, or work capital. This way you can hang in there through any slow times. Once your bills are paid off, and you have a comfortable nest egg, give yourself a small raise and start planning and saving for the home and the other beautiful things in your dreams.

The smartest salespeople I know pay cash for almost everything they purchase, other than a home. Since they are debt free, they're never affected by the ups and downs of the economy quite as bad as everyone else. If they want, or need more income, they simply look for something additional to sell. It's hard to do that when you're stuck in an eight-to-five job, working for a fixed income.

Most successful salespeople have many tricks up their sleeves, and more than just one product line to offer. The key to financial success is usually diversification, and no one is better at diversifying than a professional salesperson.

If you stick with this plan, <u>and save</u>, you can eventually build up enough money in the bank to fund each coming year's budget in advance. This includes having enough savings set aside for repairs on your car and the general maintenance of your home, clothing, medical and dental along with the next years upcoming taxes based on your average yearly income.

The first time you achieve that goal, you will truly understand what it feels like to be free! And I guarantee, you will never want to go back to the way you lived before.

William S. Crenshaw

CHAPTER 3
THE GAME OF SHOW AND TELL

If you haven't tried your hand at selling before, the idea of approaching a complete stranger and starting a conversation might sound very intimidating. However, once you have learned a few basic sales techniques you will quickly have a change of heart.

Now, you will think of each new encounter as a friendly opportunity to share something special with someone you have just met. The more you learn about the many products or services you're selling, the more you will look forward to each new sales call, and before you know it, you'll be well on your way to success.

Like anything new, discovering how to approach a client and create a desire for a product, or service, can seem extremely difficult at first. But it's possible to make the learning process easier with a simple technique I learned as a young man. The trick is to compare selling, and the art of sales, to something you

41

enjoy and have participated in many times during your life. This comparison will connect you to the learning process and help you find a selling style that fits your own unique personality.

Just to get things rolling, I will use different games like the ones we talked about in the first story for a comparison. This will show you how close the two activities, selling and playing games are. As we progress, you will start comparing sales to other thought-provoking activities, and your selling efforts will benefit from each one.

If you're hoping to become a skilled player in any game, you must first learn all you can about every aspect of the activity in which you choose to participate. When it comes to the art of sales, don't be fooled into thinking there's nothing to it.

Most hopeful newcomers in sales do not take time to learn anything. They believe that since it doesn't take a college degree to become a salesperson, it can't be very difficult. So anyone can do it, with no experience at all, right?

Now, with a giant smile plastered on their faces, and a what can I do for you today, on the tip of their tongues, these unprepared newbie's, think they can get right to it and start making the big bucks. What they haven't figured out yet, however, is there's a difference between order takers and professional salespeople, and those who don't study will only produce mediocre results at best.

The fact of the matter is, when it comes to selling, there is more to learn than you could ever imagine. In addition, like most other games, there are many different levels of expertise in which to play in or compete. That's why I say you must be willing to study your craft constantly. Only then will you have what it takes to become a dominant player.

Once you have chosen to get in the game of sales, don't go it alone. All the great masters in sales began by asking many questions. Then they read and studied the moves of their most admired predecessors. Next, they learned the rules of selling, and tricks of the trade in the category, or sales field, they chose. After that, they tweaked the process to create their own individual strategies and sales techniques, and voila, a new master was born.

Every successful salesperson will tell you, there are no short cuts to success. The harder you are willing to work and study sales, the better you will become.

Now, if you have never been involved in sales before, you will have lots of questions that need answers, so let's start at the beginning.

Surprisingly enough, almost everyone who went to school in the United States, had an introductory course in sales, and they didn't even know it. Your kindergarten teacher called it, the game of show and tell.

Many of us remember how shy we were back then, and how hard it was for us to make new friends. But our savvy teacher had figured out a way to help us break the ice and blend in with our new classmates. The key to bringing this little group of monsters all together in one place peacefully, and seeing to it that we all got along together, was knowledge. And the ingenious method she used to pull this off was teaching us how to introduce, or sell, ourselves to one another. Once we discovered a little bit about each other, our new schoolmates didn't seem so scary or weird anymore. As a matter of fact, most of them were quite interesting, and the more we knew about one another, the more apt we were to start paying attention to what others had to say. Before long, we were all friends, not strangers, and peace had prevailed.

When you stop and think about it, the same thing holds true for adults. No one is comfortable doing business with a stranger, so it is important for you to introduce yourself and become familiar with your prospective clients. Once they get to know you, they will invite you in to their inner circle, and the comfortable feeling that prevails will make the sales process much easier.

What I especially loved about that early period in my life were the unique and exciting things my classmates brought to share, and all the neat stories that accompanied them. You see storytelling was the most essential ingredient of all in the game of show and tell.

Looking back, even in kindergarten many students were blessed with the gift of gab and quite eloquent for their age. Others had an uncanny way of enhancing the truth to capture our imagination and bring us to the edge of our seats.

Some adventurous little boys went immediately for a shock and awe approach by bringing something big and scary to class, like tarantulas and gopher snakes. This brought immediate ooh's and aah's from all the kids, and certainly got the teachers attention.

There were also students who could really put on a show. They had their own distinct style when it came to presentation.

Other boys and girls played on envy appeal by bringing expensive toys and hobbies to the classroom. They used those objects to tempt, and tease the rest of us with their higher status in the community.

45

Last, but not least, were those unique kids who shared their own creations in class, and the creativity we saw in them inspired us all to do our very best. They turned out to be the true geniuses of the future, and deep down inside we all hoped we could be as special someday.

As I watched and listened to those kids in awe, I realized for the first time in my life, just how easy it was to weave a story and capture the minds of the audience. If you were well prepared, you could sway the crowd in any direction you wanted them to go.

In all, the little game our teacher had us play, called show and tell, did much more for us than she could have ever imagined. Not only did it help us get to know one another, it stirred our imagination and opened our eyes and minds, to the wonderful world of sales.

As time went on, memories from that class faded into the background, but each one of us used that lesson, in one way or another, to help us through life. You see, we all have something to sell, and it begins with the game of show and tell.

A few years later, in the sixth grade, our class was lucky enough to have a truly special instructor who helped us build our own functional radio station in class. This teacher had mastered another technique used in the game of sales and his specialty was the carrot-on-the-stick routine. In this sales pitch, the teacher worked his magic by telling everyone they could have a role in scripting, producing and performing in each radio show. However, no one could participate unless the whole class kept their grades above a "C". If everyone worked hard, and got good grades, the broadcast would be heard throughout the entire school.

By using the right incentive and creating a strong desire in all the students, he was able to obtain the exact results he wanted.

Like the kindergarten teacher before him, he also wanted us to bond together and work as a unit. By connecting all our grades together, he had killed two birds with one stone and a sale was made.

It was amazing to see how hard we all worked as a team, so we could participate in the radio show each week. If one student had problems with a subject, everyone else would come to their aid. By helping that student get their grades up, we could all be in the show. Because this teacher not only learned the art of teaching subjects, but also selling dreams, every student in his class lived up to their true potential.

One year later, I fine-tuned the game of show and tell, and used it with a formula for success my grandmother taught me just before I entered the seventh grade. I then used the combination to sell my first art project. This led to more money than a twelve-year-old kid could have ever imagined

By now, I was catching on to this thing called sales.

To me the art of sales was starting to resemble a game of chess. If I studied the board and practiced all the moves, it was possible to create strategies that would lead to predictable outcomes. This made the art of selling easy.

As I entered my teens, I soon found out how expensive it was to chase girls. To earn extra spending money, I decided to start a T-Shirt business. This soon became another educational experience in sales.

In order to move merchandise, I had to learn what marketing was all about. Then I had to advertise my products and show my potential customers what I had for sale. Since I had been saving money from my previous art endeavors, I was able to fund this enterprise, and a new sales adventure was about to begin.

Lucky for me, the kids I wanted to sell my merchandise to were trapped at school five days a week just as I was. This meant I had a captive audience. Now all I had to do was discover a way to reach out to them and advertise my cool line of T-shirts.

For my advertising campaign, I decided to go with the game of show-and-tell. I figured it was possible to recruit a small army of salespeople to show my products and sell my designs. And if I played my cards right... it wouldn't cost me a dime. All I had to do was give them complimentary T-shirts to wear while they were at school, and they would function as walking, talking billboards. Before long, my shirts were everywhere, and sales went through the roof.

As far back as I can remember, selling and the art of sales played a crucial role in my development. When I entered high school learning how to sell my ideas and talents gave me the opportunity to enjoy a rich and full life as a teenager. However, once I got out on my own, things changed quickly, and the good times disappeared.

After I graduated from high school, and started looking for employment, one of my first jobs was working as a salaried laborer, for a paint manufacturing company, in East Los Angeles.

Now, with very little money to speak of and a low paying job my fate seemed sealed, and my prospects where gloomy at best.

Because I was poor, the only place I could find to live was in the lower eastside of L.A., and that was a far cry from the nice home I lived in where I grew up. This new environment, and poor quality of life, soon had me daydreaming of other places I'd rather be. But I had a lot to learn before I could work my way out of the streets of L.A.

Since I was a big kid, I seemed well suited for heavy labor. However, I was always more interested in the business end of what was going on around me, and these city folks seemed to have more angles than you could shake a stick at.

The paint company I went to work for, not only made paint for their own retail-outlets, they also manufactured and canned paint, using custom labels, for other paint companies. Their paint was selling everywhere. But what was really weird was the fact that the same paint was selling for different prices in different stores. In most cases, the only difference was the label, and the advertising campaign they used to pitch their product. When each container looked its best, and the sales pitch was perfect, they were able to sell the same paint for a higher price. This taught me how valuable a strong sales-pitch was, and the importance of an eye-catching display or presentation. It also introduced me to different types of advertising campaigns. They called the concept, selling the sizzle, not the steak.

At that job, I started as a scrub, and then worked my way up to the canning tables. But I could not help noticing all the men and women who made the real money were the company's owners and salespeople. They wore beautiful clothes, drove shiny new cars, lived in large houses and were always talking about their dreams and what they where shooting for next.

While these salespeople were going out to lunch and diner at the finest restaurants, everyone else brought a sandwich from home, or got something from the roach-coach when it pulled up in front of the building. This division of wealth, between the company's sales team and the rest of us, drove the point home fast about the difference of hourly paychecks and open-ended commissions.

If you weren't a salesperson, being paid commission, you were a salaried employee and lived paycheck-to-paycheck. This locked you into a fixed income, and you were always hurting for money.

When I tried to talk to the other salaried employees about their dreams, they would just shrug their shoulders and say, "Hey, I gave up on my dreams a long time ago. Once I was married, I traded them in for job security and a steady paycheck. Now, I have a

51

family to take care of, and I don't have time to dream anymore."

To me that was the saddest thing I had ever heard.

The two words, fixed and dreams, definitely didn't go together, and no job security, or steady paycheck, was worth trading your dreams for. Life was too short, and I was too young to feel trapped like that.

When I found myself disillusioned with salaried jobs, the idea of selling my talent again sounded like a good idea, and the game of show and tell would come in handy once more. However, this time I knew I would need to add an adult twist to the formula. Moving forward, I would be playing for larger sums of money and the retail market place would become my next source of inspiration.

This is when I chose to dream about the design field, and retail sales. I could just imagine how much fun it would be to have a beautiful new apartment, in a nice part of town, and decorate it like some of the places I had seen in the movies, and magazines. This fascination with beautiful home furnishings and accessories became a mental escape for me and took me far away from the gunshots ringing out in my neighborhood each night.

Later on, that same obsession would become my ticket out of the city and into the life I dreamed of.

The people in the streets of L.A. were different from the small agricultural community I had grown up in, and the different types of sales opportunities were mind blowing, to say the least.

Back in my hometown, people called it like it was. Price dickering and hustles were not commonplace there, but now I had a lot to learn about buying and selling in a diversified metropolitan area.

In L.A., each nationality went about selling their products differently, and the people who lived there were used to doing business with them in that fashion. But this meant newcomers, and outsiders, had to become better buyers, smarter and more knowledgeable about the actual prices each product should bring. In East Los Angeles, price dickering was a way of life and the selling game was about to get a lot more interesting.

If you were a merchant in that area, you had to increase your prices. Then you had to have a preset limit as to just how far you would be willing to drop them, before an item would be unprofitable to sell. When you shopped there, you had to remember, all sticker prices were fictional. Only suckers paid those prices.

In this setting... like in a poker game, you had to learn how to keep your emotions in check. If the merchant knew, or was suspicious about how much you wanted something, he had the upper hand and could bluff you into buying the item for a higher price. However, if you were good at acting indifferent, like you weren't interested, you could sometimes walk away with a steal. Win, lose or draw, it was all in the bluff. Just like poker, this was another part of the selling game.

On the other hand, if you were a merchant, selling things other than basic commodities, such as a one-of-a kind item, you could bluff and shoot for the moon price wise. Then all you had to do was find a customer that just had to have those items, and you could make a killing.

Overall it was fascinating to see how different parts of the city showcased, and presented their products.

In the poorest parts of town, you had unsavory characters hustling merchandise from the trunks of their cars, and street vendors hocking merchandise out in the open.

In this area, you would also find used-furniture stores, junk shops, so-called wholesale outlets, featuring knock-off merchandise, and garage sales. If you shopped in any of these places, they use to say, let the buyer beware.

When you traveled farther uptown there were retail stores and antique shops all packed with goods, but most of them were dimly lit and poorly maintained, and the sales clerks offered customers little or no help at all.

However, when you came to Rodeo Drive, and the Beverly Hills area, you saw every kind of product imaginable on display and merchandising and presentation was at its best. In this high-dollar area, the merchants and salespeople really knew how to romance their customers.

In these fine shops, there was no disheveled merchandise on the shelves. Instead of walking down poorly lit isles on dirty floors, it took your breath away to see the floors shine and the items sparkle. Further more, price dickering was unacceptable.

These classy storeowners had turned the art of sales, and shopping, into an unforgettable experience so they didn't have to play lets make a deal with their prices. When people shopped there, not only were they comfortable paying the asking price for any item... they bragged about it to their friends. Just to be seen strolling down Rodeo Drive, with a Neiman Marcus logo on your shopping bag, was a badge of honor.

During this period in my life, I was fortunate to have had a chance to see, and experience, retail sales in every conceivable form. And it didn't take long for me to choose where I wanted to be.

If you choose to sell low-end merchandise, you have to sell a ton of goods to make a decent living, and playing the price game, and dickering is something you had better like to do.

However, selling high-end products offered anyone a chance to shoot for the moon, and even if you fall short, you might land on a star. A wise man once said, "that sure beats being stuck down here on earth with everyone else."

Now, to start my career in sales, all I had to do was come up with a plan and stick to it!

By this time, I had become fascinated with the field of interior design, but it required four years of college before you could get a degree and become a licensed interior designer. But as you probably already guessed, I didn't let that stop me. Since I hated school, and was determined to break into that field, I used the plan I shared with you in the first chapter and got in through the backdoor.

After choosing which subject I wanted to sell, I learned everything about it. Then I chose a number of areas I would like to live in, and started going out on field trips. Not long after that I found a job opportunity working at a retail furniture store and became a decorator. That job was just what I had been dreaming of, and I started earning a great income almost immediately.

Interior designers needed four years of college and specialized training before they could become licensed and work for a design studio, or home furnishings outlet. Then, after spending four years in school and accumulating debt, through student loans, they still had to go out and look for a job, just like everyone else. But I didn't need a degree to work as a decorator in a high-end furniture store. In that environment, I was able to sell the most beautiful furniture and accessories in the world, to the richest customers in the city, and I was debt free!

Ironically, I was paid the same commission for all my sales that the snooty interior designers received. All the customers truly cared about was my talent and how well I took care of them.

Now it was time for me to turn the game of show and tell into a moneymaking art form, and start cashing in on it. You see half the job of selling, is story telling. The other half is learning how to create a desire for the item you wish to sell by showing it in a most desirable way.

57

Within a few months, after I landed that job, I quadrupled my yearly income and was well on my way to success. Three years later, I was offered 45% interest in a beautiful new 16,000 square foot design studio. Because of my unique sales and design capabilities, that partnership didn't cost me a dime.

William S. Crenshaw

CHAPTER 4
PREPARING FOR SUCCESS

In Chapter 2, I talked to you about how important it is for an up-and-coming salesperson to prepare for financial success. You do that by staying debt-free, creating a spending plan, and living within a budget.

You must also prepare for a successful career in sales in much the same way. First, you have to decide what you would like to sell. Are you interested in wholesale, retail, or outside sales?

Then you must think about what you hope to achieve in the long run. Do you want to work for someone else the rest of your life, and let them carry all the responsibility of running the business and paying the bills? Or do you hope to own your own business some day?

Next, you want to think about how tied down you want to be to a business. Some retail businesses have to maintain a huge inventory, and work fixed hours, or shifts. When you combine long hours and all that merchandise with overseeing personnel, owning your own business can become an anchor around your neck.

But other types of businesses carry no inventory at all and offer very flexible hours.

As you can clearly see, there is a lot to think about when it comes to preparing for success in sales.

After thinking about all that, you need to sit down and write a plan that lists what you want to achieve in your life. This plan will help you chart a course for your sales career. Once you have decided what your short-term goals are, place them in the order you hope to achieve them in and prioritize your lifetime hopes and dreams close behind those. Then stick with the plan. You can accomplish anything you set out to do, one-step at a time.

Next, if you want to become an outstanding salesperson, you have to develop a mindset for it. You know who you are right now, but who would you honestly like to be? Once you discover that, it is time for you to reinvent yourself, and start building the future of your dreams.

This might sound like a challenge; however, there are many fun ways to get the job done.

When it comes to financial prosperity, and learning how to prepare a budget, few people offer better advice than the radio and television talk show host, and best selling author, Dave Ramsey. However, when it comes to getting your psyche and sales pitches in order, it is hard to beat watching a good movie or reading a classic book. But don't get me wrong. I am not talking about the newest copy of, "how to become the richest salesperson in the world overnight." Or a sales pitch pep-talk video created by the latest, greatest sales guru. I am referring to a good old classic movie like, "Miracle on 34th Street", or a newer film sensation featuring Will Smith in, "The Pursuit of Happiness."

Documentaries on the founders of such well known companies as; J.C. Penny, Sears and Roebuck, Hershey, and Heinz, also show how common people with dreams and determination started with nothing, and built some of Americas most impressive businesses by selling simple, everyday retail products.

Other feature films, and biography's, such as Pirates of Silicone Valley, The Social Network, and The Oracle of Omaha will give you a behind the scenes look at some of America's best-known figures. Steve Jobs, Bill Gates, Mark Zuckerberg, and Warren Buffet, all began with nothing. Yet they wound up becoming

63

some of the richest people in the world, due to their abilities to sell their ideas and visions of the future.

If dreams of grandeur aren't your thing, there are more down to earth books and movies that will inspire you with the deeds of ordinary everyday people, who did small things in great ways. To me these stories made some of the most inspiring films of all. <u>Coco Chanel</u>, <u>Mildred Pierce</u>, and the <u>Greatest Game Ever Played</u> are all inspirational stories that show what common people with guts and determination can do.

By watching these incredible movies, you will come to realize that many of the world's most successful people didn't have a college education. And some of them came from families that were as poor as church mice, but they all possessed the three most valuable things of all; hope, faith, and dreams. With this can-do spirit and a little guidance, you can become successful too!

Most importantly, however, you must learn how to watch these movies and read each book through the eyes of a salesperson.

If you watch movies, and read books as most people do, all you are getting out of it is the entertainment value. But a talented salesperson learns how to get something enlightening out of every story. There are hundreds of things going on behind the scenes for you to notice if you learn how to look deeper and make parallel comparisons between the movies you are watching and your own real life. Any, or all, of these situations can inspire you.

Writers and Moviemakers, are the masters of invention, and actors bring their stories to life. Compare that scenario to your career in sales, then think of designers and manufacturing companies as the masters of industry. And salespeople bring their dreams of selling their products to life.

What I find fascinating is the fact that every successful person is playing a part in the game of life. The mere fact that they are successful is proof that they have picked the perfect role for themselves, and invented a believable character to portray.

When I was growing up, my two favorite actors were John Wayne, and Cary Grant. It surprised me to learn that everything about them was invented. The way they walked, talked, even their names were created to capture a certain persona that would be looked upon with favor by the audience they would be reaching out to, and boy did it work!

One of them was rugged and outspoken and seldom took any crap from anyone. His word was his bond, and he could back up anything he said with a good, right cross to the jaw if you got out of line. To

65

solidify that image and fit in with every man, he talked slowly and walked with a certain swagger. This man, who we know as John Wayne, became the character he invented, and we idolized him. In order to realize just how important it was for our hero to reinvent himself, try picturing him using his real name ... Marion Morrison. No matter how hard you try, the hero and his sir name just will not connect.

My second hero epitomized the very essence of class and sophistication, but he was not born into it. His real name was Archibald Alexander Leach. However, we know him as Cary Grant.

Born in Bristol, England, in 1904, Archibald Leach was brought up in a lower middle class home, in one of the tougher parts of the UK. There, he developed a Cockney accent, and suffered significant set backs during his childhood after his mother was placed in a mental institution. But In 1920, at the age of 16, he made his way to the United States and decided to reinvent himself. Once again, everything that made him who he was had to change. After he had changed his name to Cary Grant, he decided the image of a tough guy, and the Cockney accent had to go. He knew this was his chance to become anyone he wanted to be, and the classy, sophisticated movie sets, and wealthy socialites of Hollywood inspired him to play the role of a debonair man-about-town. In order to pull this off, and make it believable, he had to become the essence of the make-believe character he envisioned in his mind.

Imagine if you can, coming here from another country and changing everything there is about yourself, to become the person that you would truly like to be. He did just that.

First, he changed the way he combed his hair, then the way he dressed, and the manner in which he spoke. Next, he changed his accent and took etiquette lessons. Then he worked on developing his knowledge about the finer things in life and started patterning himself after the most sophisticated people he could find. After that, he invented the character we know as Cary Grant.

Many years later, when he had become one of the original Super Stars of the 20th Century, an interviewer told him, "Everyone would like to be Cary Grant." He responded by saying, "So would I."

One of the key things that most successful people have figured out, which sets them apart from everyone else, is the fact that they don't have to stay the way they are at this very moment in time. They have the ability to reinvent themselves. And once they learn how, there is no stopping them.

67

While there are hundreds, if not thousands, of inspirational movies to watch that connect with reinventing yourself, one in particular really stood out when I watched it recently. That film was, "Vidal Sassoon, The Movie." The sub title read... "How one man changed the world with a pair of scissors." However, what the New York Times was quoted as saying captured the essence of the biography. They said, "This movie isn't just the story of a brilliant fashion idea that swept the globe. It is a euphoric account of one man's strenuous self-invention." And in my opinion, it is amazing!

I'm embarrassed to say that I almost overlooked the opportunity to watch this magnificent film. I thought it was probably just another chick-flick, but I can't tell you how many times I've been wrong in that regard. This movie was so much more than just a story about one of the world's greatest hair stylists. It was a systematic guide to figuring out what your talent is, and whom you want to be, then it shows you how to make it happen.

As I watched the movie, it brought memories back about figuring out what I wanted to be when I was just a kid, and how I reinvented myself the first time. That successful endeavor was unbelievable, but I was so young I really did not understand what made it work. A few years later, after I was able to make the formula work the second time around, I learned how to use the process at will, and it made all my dreams come true.

By now, it should be clear how much information you could glean from a good movie or book. With all the movie titles there are to choose from, and the special videos created for the Biography Network on Cable TV, there is a treasure trove of subjects to choose from that will inspire you.

Next time you think how incredible life could be if only you could reinvent yourself, remember ... Hollywood has created an army of make believe characters to bring their movies to life, and the public has responded by spending billions of dollars at the box office to watch them perform.

Literally, millions of dollars, and thousands of man-hours are spent making a single movie, and we can watch each one, or own it, for just a few dollars.

What is even more exciting is the fact that every one of these incredible films is filled with words of wisdom, and secondary plots, which will aid you in building strategies for your own once-in-a-life time encounters.

Since the early 1900s, reading books and watching movies has been a never-ending source of both information, and inspiration for people who have made a career in sales. Through books and movies, we have witnessed some of the greatest sales pitches of all time being delivered in unforgettable ways.

On the giant silver screen, we have seen men, women, and children alike, drop hints, bat their eyes, and reach for the stars in an effort to obtain their hearts desire, and the results usually ended up with a sale being made.

Since many of the finest books and movies we have indulged ourselves in have been based on true stories, the content had played a significant role in making us believe that we can do anything when we put our minds to it. What one man can do ... another can do, it is all in a state of mind.

Now we know that no matter who you are, where you live, or how old you are, every human being can learn how to play a game, tell a story, and make a sale. All you have to do is become fascinated with something, learn everything you can about it, and weave that information into a captivating story.

When you do, you will find the public will love hearing you tell your tale. Story telling is fun if you know what you are talking about, and the whole world is your stage when you are in sales.

After reading a few exceptional books and watching some inspirational movies, I hope you start dreaming of a different you. Become someone with a bright future that knows no bounds, who can't wait to jump out of bed each day ready to make your fortune.

Now, before you start looking for a job, the next thing I want you to do is to sit down with a piece of paper and an ink pen, or your computer, and prepare a plan for your future. One of the most remarkable phenomena's in life is the power of the written word. One of its greatest assets is the strength those words give to the ones who write them down. **However, don't just say you'll do it, do it now!**

Mouthing the words will not get the job done, and there are no excuses for being lazy.

Procrastination is a weakness found in the personality of most wannabe salespeople and non-achievers. It is the single most common obstacle in your path to success. So do not fall prey to it!

When you begin your list of things to do, start by critiquing yourself and do not be kind.

Successful salespeople are their own worst critics. They do not lie to themselves, cheat themselves or steal from themselves, and they eventually wind up becoming their own best friends. If you cannot believe in yourself, then whom can you believe in.

When you begin the critique process, start the same way Archibald Leach, or Cary Grant did. Look at yourself in the mirror and be honest. Is that who you truly want to be? If not, make changing your appearance number one on your list.

Next, write down what you think would help you look your best and remember, you're not trying to become a model, but you don't want to look like a slob either. At this stage of the game, most people appear to be a little rough around the edges, but everyone has a certain look that suits them. The trick is discovering it.

Since we are not all designers, it makes sense that we need help to find our style. Cary Grant hired a stylist who created his look, and it paid big dividends. Once your style suits you, and you're exercising regularly and watching your diet, you want to dress accordingly. After doing these things, you won't believe how much more self-confidence you will have, and everyone you come in contact with will see it and feel it too!

Next, check out the way you walk and talk. Do you have good posture and are you carrying yourself properly. Or do you tend to slouch, or shuffle when you walk, and use poor language, or grammar, when you talk? That is an instant turn off to employers and customers alike!

Many people unknowingly pick up some of the characteristics and bad habits of the crowd they hang around. That's what happened to young Archibald Leach. Then, before he knew it, he resembled them. But that is something you can change if you really want to succeed in life, the same way he did.

If anything is worth doing, it's worth doing right. Imagine how much more believable you will be, when you go out looking for a job, if you not only look great, but carry yourself with style and grace and talk properly. This effort could be worth a small fortune to you in the years to come.

After that, it wouldn't hurt for you to put some effort into broadening your horizons. Learn the difference between average and high quality merchandise. Wealthy people are taught the difference between low-end and high-end products from the time they are in their teens, if not before, and most sophisticated adults know quality when they see it. If you want to fit in with the people you intend on doing business with, or at least not look out of place, it will pay you to start asking as many questions as possible. Inquire about the quality in home furnishings and accessories, clothes, cars, jewelry, china, wines, foods, restaurants, vacation spots, architecture, music and everything else you can think of. This knowledge will come in handy the rest of your life.

One last thought ... if you're smart you will leave politics and personal likes, and dislikes, out of your conversations. You want to be like a chameleon, able to blend in comfortably with any group of people, and any situation.

As you watch and learn different angles for making sales pitches and start practicing your delivery, you should also pay attention to the reasons most people, including yourself, show loyalty to one salesperson over another. When I figured that out, it changed everything about the way I approached each customer, and I've been rewarded handsomely for my efforts ever since.

I have always believed that people could acquire almost any of the same goods they bought from me, somewhere else. But the reason they chose me as their salesperson, rather than another, was that I made the buying experience fun, and enlightening.

I feel each customer should be courted and romanced so they know how special they are. We all like being appreciated and we love picking up helpful tidbits of information along the way. When we are pleased with a salesperson's courtesy, helpfulness, and knowledge, we are most likely to return that favor with our loyalty and repeat business. This is how you build a following and establish yourself as a leader in the field of sales. But first, you have to find a job.

Learning how to make a sale is a never-ending process, and you are not just pitching a sale when you are trying to sell a customer a product, or service. You are also trying to land a sale when you look for a job. The best way to do this is to keep thinking to yourself, a sale is a sale, no matter what you're pitching. If you are going to make anything happen in this life, it all begins by making a sale.

When you are searching for a job, you want to remember employers need to be treated just like customers, and they will respond in the same manner by offering you an opportunity. Business owners find it refreshing to be courted by a polite, knowledgeable salesperson that shows a sincere interest in their company, and most businesspeople are constantly looking for new talent.

Because the same scenarios hold true whether you are selling a product, or yourself, the movies you watch and books you read will click in your mind, and help you think in a positive way.

Now, that you have created the perfect you, developed your sales techniques, and studied the subject you picked, it is time for you to hit the streets

75

and start frequenting the places where you would like to work. And whatever you do, don't forget to dream!

Dream big, and then choose the neatest place to work for you can imagine and shoot for the moon! Do not be timid or shy. After all, what do you have to lose? They cannot do anything to you worse than saying ... sorry, but we do not have any openings at this time. Remember, you have the odds in your favor. All you have to do is find one opening, get your foot in the door, and your life could change forever, just as it did for me.

When you visit a business that you are intrigued with, ask questions and show desire. Then let the people you talk with know how interested you are in having an opportunity to work there. Next, state that you are willing to start in any position, and never go unprepared. Always be ready to tell an interesting story about yourself, and anxious to answer any questions. You should also have a well-written resume with you at all times that will include a good picture of yourself, not a goofy snapshot! Don't take shortcuts! Get it professionally done. You are sincere about becoming successful, or you are not, and what you leave behind will prove how serious you are!

In your resume, be sure to point out that your main goal is to work in sales. Clearly state that you prefer to work for commission, rather than a flat salary. This is a win-win situation for you and most employers. If you don't sell anything, they aren't out any money, so they have nothing to lose. But if you are skilled at your job, you will earn twice as much as you could have ever hoped for, especially if you were only paid an hourly wage.

Always remember, everyone's first concern is, what's in it for me, and employers are no exception.

This approach will give you, and your new boss, a risk-free chance to take a leap of faith with one another. The rest is up to you. The more you sell, the more you can earn, and believe me, when it comes to commission checks ... the sky is the limit!

William S. Crenshaw

CHAPTER 5
PRODUCT KNOWLEDGE

Once you land a job in sales, your earnings will be directly related to how much knowledge you have about the objects you are trying to sell. Another key factor will be how well you have adjusted to your new surroundings.

Up until now, you worked to learn general information about everything of interest to you. Then you used that knowledge to get your foot in the door and find a job.

Now, that you have found an opportunity to work in sales, do not settle into a rut. This is when the real work should begin.

Your next challenge should be learning specifics about everything there is to sell in this new environment. Perhaps the business that hired you manufactures the products you will be selling and sells them wholesale, to retail storeowners. Or maybe you have been hired by a retail sales-outlet. In that case, you will be selling the products the storeowner purchased for resale, to the public or end user.

You might also have found a job as an outside salesperson working for an advertising agency. In that case, your job could involve selling the same product to both the wholesale clients and the retail customers combined. In either case your need for more information has just taken a quantum leap forward. So it is time for you to start the question and answer phase of your new job and build up all the knowledge you can acquire.

After that, work on developing interesting stories filled with insightful tidbits of helpful information about each item. Next, you want to learn the rhythm and flow of using that information in your conversations with customers. And do not forget, you must become familiar with your new place of business and learn what is going on all around you.

Customers will base your worth on the amount of knowledge you possess, and how quickly you can answer their questions.

Sales had played a vital role in my life beginning when I was just 12 years old, so everything I see or hear makes me start to think of the perfect lead-in to a well-rounded sales pitch. Every word or gesture a customer follows up with, after my opening statement, is like music to my ears. And each time I hear a vague rejection, I think of an impressive comeback I can use that will help us see eye-to-eye, then the sale is mine!

To me, the art of selling is a mind game with strategies much like chess, and a good player rehearses every predictable move in advance. Since there is a counter for each move you make, any serious player will tell you, it takes a lot of preparation, and practice, to overcome a blocked move, or rejection, with the perfect comeback. Once you have developed your product knowledge, along with a series of diversified responses for every conceivable rejection, you will be ready to make more sales.

Woody Allen once said, "Just showing up is half of winning, " but he never said what the other half of the equation was.

When it comes to closing sales, I believe just showing up is the first half of winning, but the most essential ingredient for success is the second half ... preparation and product knowledge.

If you show up in the right place, at the right time, with all the right information, you are an odds-on-favorite to make the sale and be a winner.

I know that I will have many opportunities to make a sale each day if I am prepared. Because of that belief, I am constantly studying everything around me. When the opportunity to make a sale presents itself, I can quickly recall that information at a moment's notice and move in to close the sale.

I also understand the fact that you only get one chance to make a good first impression, and the same is true when it comes to making a sale... I am ready to make a sale today, are you?

If you want to become a great salesperson, you should always begin by building up your product knowledge. You can't sell what you don't know, and no one wants to give you time to figure out what's available, and how much the asking price is, when they're ready to make a purchase.

Order-takers give salespeople a bad name. Just because they make a sale now and then, does not make an order-taker a real salesperson. Even a blind groundhog finds an acorn every once in a while, but stumbling and fumbling around for answers will cost order-takers more sales than they will ever make. What makes this scenario even worse, is that if you are an order-taker, your inability to help a customer will make them doubt not only you, but also the store you work for, and they may never return.

Most order-takers love to talk with people, and they think that will be the key to their success, but you have to remember that the average customer will not be coming to visit with you. They will most likely have a specific need they hope you can fill. Since they are searching for something in particular, they hope you can answer their questions quickly and help them find it. When you are knowledgeable and able to answer their questions immediately the customer will build up confidence in you, and the sale will be yours. They will also keep coming back to the store and the salesperson that has all the right answers.

It is fun to make sales when you know what you are doing, and you are ready for whatever pops up. As your product knowledge grows, so will your income. The wealthiest people in sales are always the ones who are the best prepared.

It's funny what a small world this is and how many times each day the question and answer scenario plays out.

Just as I sat down to write about the importance of product knowledge, my shop supervisor called me to say one of our small, work trucks had broken down. He thought we should buy a new one. The idea seemed unanimous, after talking to my bookkeeper, so I decided to buy a new pickup over the weekend.

When Saturday morning came, the first thing I did was check online to find out what companies made

83

small trucks and where the price ranges started. Now I had an idea of what a basic, small truck sold for, around $18,000, before any necessary fees and sales tax, so I thought I could buy a new truck in a matter of hours. Boy was I mistaken! Trying to get someone to help me over the phone was like pulling teeth.

The first mistake that many a wannabe salesperson makes, is thinking someone making a telephone inquiry is probably just a waste of their time. In my case, like many of my friends, I work long hours and don't have a lot of time to roam around window-shopping. Instead, I do some quick looking on the Internet to get my bearings straight. Then I hit the telephone hoping to find a knowledgeable salesperson. Next, I expect to find out if the dealership I have called, has the make and model truck I want in stock, and what approximate price they would be willing to sell it for. If the salesperson can answer those questions and makes me feel comfortable on the telephone, he or she is half way to closing the sale and making a nice commission check.

If, on the other hand, they are not ready to answer those questions, and they tell me that they need to take my phone number, so they can get back to me with that information, they have probably lost the sale.

In my case, what this salesperson failed to understand was the fact that if he could answer my questions while I was on the phone, I was ready to jump in my car and head straight to his showroom. Since he was unable to, I called another dealership the minute we hung up.

While the first salesman was trying to find answers to my questions, that he should have already known, the new sales rep I was talking to, at another dealership was prepared, and he answered all of my questions immediately. And you guessed it... he got the sale.

When I was a young man, in my early twenties, I had a good friend that worked for the Buick-Pontiac dealership in the town where I grew up. He was their number one salesman, and he sold so many cars that he started buying real estate with the commissions he made. Eventually he became financially independent.

When I asked him how he sold so many automobiles each month he said, "After I began working for the dealership I started hanging around at all different times of the day and night, not just when I was paid to be there. In fact, I was around so much of the time that some of the staff members started teasing me by calling me the new company mascot.

85

When I was there, I spent time not only on the sales floor and out in the lot, but also in the office behind the scenes, and in the maintenance, service and parts department. I wanted to learn everything there was to know about the business.

Before long, I noticed that everyone I knew loved to eat at a Chinese restaurant two doors down from the car lot. With that in mind, I thought to myself, after eating a tasty meal, most people like to stretch their legs. And what better way is there to do that than to walk next door to the automobile dealership and check out the most beautiful new cars in town?

Next, I asked the boss if I could work every Friday and Saturday nights, and he said, "Sure, that's when everyone else wants off, so you would be doing me a big favor." From that moment on, I had the perfect set up. All I had to do then was memorize everything there was to know about every car we had on the lot and stake my claim to the corner.

After that, I made it a personal challenge to find out the names of all the regulars that came to eat at the restaurant next door. Then I started inviting them over to the car lot to see our hottest new models and take them for a test drive after dinner. It was unbelievable how comfortable a potential customer was, after having a satisfying meal. It's easy, at that time, to get them to look at a new car. It also never hurt for the husband to see his beautiful wife sitting behind the steering wheel of a brand new Buick. The rest is history."

As we continued talking he said, "When I started working at the car lot, even though I had done my best to prepare for answering anything that would be asked of me, I knew someone would hit me with a question I wasn't ready for. To make sure I was never caught off guard twice by the same question, I wrote each one down. Then I found the answer and memorized it.

Many of the questions customers asked were always answered with an instant no, by other salespeople and management, but those same questions intrigued me. So I took it upon myself to see if I could satisfy everyone on my own. If the manufacturing company and the dealership could not, or did not want to get involved with my customers unusual request, that didn't mean I had to say no.

Some of my customer's most common questions were, "I love the car, but do you have the same model with a white leather interior. If you don't, could you order it for me with that custom upholstery"?

Now I already knew that the manufacturer did not offer the car with that interior, and the dealership did not want to get involved. But why couldn't I make a deal with an upholsterer and customize the inside of the car myself?

With that in mind, I went on a field trip and checked out all the upholstery shops in a sixty-mile radius. It did not take long to find the one that offered the best quality work at an affordable rate.

Next the upholsterer and I worked out a price on some custom leather interiors, and I made a deal with him to do all of my interior conversions.

Customers also asked me about having custom paint jobs and pin striping on their new cars, so I made a deal with a local artist and custom paint and body shop and added that to my list of extra services, and the list went on."

With each custom option, my friend added to his repertoire, his commissions kept growing. It wasn't long until he had checks coming in from everywhere. In short, what made him so successful in the automobile business was the fact that he made it his mission to give the customer anything they wanted. He always said yes, instead of no. He also gave each customer the chance to dream big and have the time of their lives spending their money.

Many salesmen worked at that dealership through the years, but no one ever sold half as many cars as my friend did. If you called him on the telephone and asked him questions about anything, he could answer your questions immediately. Because of his product knowledge, thoughtfulness and wonderful personality, he became so popular that his customers wouldn't talk to anyone else but him. If they came in looking for a new car and he wasn't there, they would just leave and come back later.

You could buy a new car from someone else, but why would you? This guy never let you down!

Eventually he retired, and lived the rest of his days off the rental income he brought in from his real estate investments, and he owed it all to product knowledge. That's what made him a top-notch salesman and exceptionally well to do!

In the sales world, things are constantly changing, but no matter what you are selling, or where you are selling it, one thing remains the same. Customers are faced with the need to know and they hope a can-do person will give them the answers.

A skilled salesperson goes into each new situation with a positive attitude and looks for all of the yeses instead of the noes. Next, they pay attention to their customer's questions to learn what they have been looking for. If they don't have it in stock, and the company they're working for doesn't carry it, they find out where they can get it, or at least the best possible knock-off available. Then they get ready for the next customer that asks about it.

A good salesperson never says, I'm sorry. We do not carry that! Or, sorry, I can't help you.

If you are a top-notch salesperson, the word "no" is not in your vocabulary, and sorry means that you have done something wrong. If you handle things right, you should never have to say you're sorry.

If the item you're looking for is not available to you, and you can't find anything like it, you should at least find out the closest store in your area that has it for sale and refer your customers there. By doing so, you will have made a friend, and they will come back when they need something else.

Don't forget... Customers keep coming back to the same store because of your product knowledge. Once they figure out that you have what they want, or know where they can get it, you will be the first one they come back to for everything they need. If you become the key source of information in your area, your competitors won't stand a chance of outselling you.

After you build up your product knowledge, start working on your approach and the delivery of your sales pitches. Begin by coming up with the perfect greeting and remember many salespeople lose their chance to make a sale the minute they say hello.

Most customers have the feeling that they are going to be stocked by a salesperson, so they are uncomfortable just saying hi, and that creates an uneasy feeling right out of the gate.

To make matters even worse, many of those same customers have been let down by so many unknowledgeable order-takers, and desk clerks, that they are almost numb when it comes to giving you the opportunity to help them. But if you play your cards right, they will be your customers for life. It all depends on the way you court them. This factor determines whether you are ready to make a sale today. Or, you just think you are!

Like my friend, the car salesman, if you want to be successful in sales, you must first develop your product knowledge and then find a comfortable way to greet new customers. You don't want to scare them off, or intimidate them, but you can't ignore them either.

Next, discover your company's strong points and share them with all of your customers. When a sales representative shows pride in the company he or she works for, it will make the customer feel safe in doing business with them.

91

After that, make sure that you are taking care of yourself by getting enough rest. It's important that you stay in excellent shape.

Most salespeople, who don't get enough rest, seem like they hate their jobs and could care less about helping a customer. It's sad to say, in many cases the only reason they appear that way is because they are tired and not quite themselves.

The same thing holds true when you let yourself go and get out of shape. A conscientious salesperson does not want to develop a sloppy, disheveled appearance. If you don't care about the way you look, and you're sagging, bagging, and dragging through the day, you're fighting an up hill battle when it comes to developing a good rapport with a new customer.

Make sure that you always put your best foot forward. Every effort you are willing to put into gaining more product knowledge and upgrading your appearance will pay you big dividends in the years to come.

Lastly, when it comes to making sure that you are ready and prepared to make a sale, you must learn how to position yourself. You need to learn how to be in the right place, at the right time!

Most people think that it is all about being lucky. However, if you study the situation, it's remarkable how certain salespeople seem to be in that lucky position more often than anyone else? The reason for that is simple! They have learned how to read the sales territory and plot a strategy for connecting with their prospective customers. They do that much the same way my friend, the car salesman did.

The art of positioning, is something I mastered by the time I was in high school, and I have been able to cash in on the technique ever since.

Positioning is something that many fathers and grandfathers taught their sons and grandsons, with hunting and fishing lessons when they were just children. Little did they know, those simple words of wisdom would help them earn their fortunes through sales, when they grew up.

Positioning also plays a crucial role in many of the games you play that require strategies like, poker and chess. This skill is an important part of a winner's hand.

In the field of sales, learning to position yourself literally means the difference between barely making a living for your sales efforts, or becoming wealthy. Once you thoroughly understand how to make the practice of positioning work, you will wind up using it in almost everything you do the rest of your life.

After you have done all this, in preparation for your next sales encounter, you will truly be ready to make a sale.

Now it's time to go out there and sell something.

William S. Crenshaw

CHAPTER 6

PLANT A SEED AND GROW A SALE

I've always loved comparisons, and my favorite teacher was my grandmother who enjoyed telling stories and talking to me in parables. She was an incredible salesperson in her own right, and her specialty was selling me a can-do spirit and belief that I could make all my dreams come true.

She has been gone for some time now, but all of her tales stay near and dear to my heart.

One of my favorite short stories she shared with me was built around an observation that connected farming, sales and faith. I can still remember the look in her eyes as she said, "I see you pace the floor as you worry about a project you're involved in right now." Then she proceeded to say, "You know, being a salesperson is a lot like being a farmer. Both of you have to till the soil and prepare it for the seeds you will sow, and it doesn't hurt to mix-in a little steer manure to fertilize the plants. Next, you have to plant the seeds

97

with care and nurture them while they grow. After that, you must have faith knowing that you did your job right and the seeds will bear fruit. Once you've done that, every successful farmer knows the rewards for his hard work, patience, and faith will be well worth it in the end. That's what has made America the most productive farming nation in the world."

Then she went on to say, "Just imagine someone who didn't understand farming trying to grow a crop. First, he would pick out a piece of farmland and get a loan from the bank for the property, seed, and supplements. Next, he would work the soil, plant the seeds and go to sleep where he would dream of the crops growing through the night. In the morning, he would jump out of bed and run outside to see the leafy plants sprouting up through the soil and, WHAM! There would be nothing in sight but the same empty fields that were there the night before when he went to bed.

At that moment, a great feeling of emptiness would overcome him, and he would feel as though he had toiled in vain.

You see, without knowledge and faith, all anyone has to fall back on is fear."

After that, she asked, "Why are you worrying? You are incredibly talented, and more knowledgeable about your profession than most others in your field. So have faith in what you've done. Be patient while you wait, and you'll soon reap the rewards of your labor!"

At that time, I was in the furniture business and my partner and I were in the middle of building a 16,000 square feet design studio called Key West Designs.

As my grandmother saw it, we were busy preparing the soil for the seeds we were about to plant. And looking back, she was absolutely right. The huge building project was our field of dreams, and we were preparing it for the crop of furniture and accessories we would be planting in the spring. We were also spreading a lot of bull around town about how incredible the new store was going to be. But she realized I was nervous about the giant monetary investment that was being plowed into this enterprise. She also knew how anxious I was, to find out if the new design studio would be profitable when it opened, and once more, her words of encouragement rang out loud and clear.

Just like the farmer, I needed to be patient and keep the faith. That faith in my ability as a designer, buyer, and top-notch-salesperson, would have to see me, and my partner through to the stores grand opening. Then we would reap our rewards.

99

From the time I was eleven years old, my grandmother had been planting seeds in my mind, and she was a master when it came to using this passive-sales-technique. Now I was about to find out how successful this subtle method of selling could be. You see, I had landed my partnership, and 45% interest in the company's stock, by planting a tiny seed in the fertile mind of my new partner just a few months earlier.

Now that seed was growing into one of the most awesome design studios in Central California, and just like my grandmother had said, all it took was hard work to develop my talent, a dream to sell, and faith when I started planting the seeds.

Through the years, I have learned that there are all kinds of sales techniques to choose from including the good, the bad and the ugly. What's interesting is the fact that each different style, or sales technique, seems to fit the personality of the salesperson who uses it.

Some salespeople are impatient, and they often use high-pressure techniques to try to close a sale fast. That aggressive approach usually signifies the salesperson is either dishonest, financially in distress, or unsure of how solid their connection is with their client. In any case, when a high-pressure sales approach is used, it's easy to see that all the salesperson is interested in is parting you from your money. This behavior brings about all the wrong feelings and gives the customer the creeps. This high-pressure technique is too pushy for me.

The mere thought of a high-pressure salesman brings to mind a slick, slimy, snake in the grass, just laying in wait for an unsuspecting customer to pass by. That vision changes the image of a potentially happy customer into an unhappy victim, and this has always been something I personally despise. You never want to pounce on a customer when they enter your store. No one likes to be ambushed!

Next, you have the 'I'm your buddy approach.' Salespeople who use this sales technique have such a huge smile plastered on their faces that it reminds me of a clown without the face paint, and that approach tends to make me a little nervous.

If you stop and think about it, a new customer who just walked into your store doesn't actually know you. This is probably the first time you have ever met. So give them a break, and don't knock them down at the front door or try to smile them into submission when you first meet. It's your job to make them feel at ease within the first few minutes that they enter the store, so tone it down a bit.

Another loosing sales technique is the snooty and oftentimes comical air-of-superiority approach.

In this salespersons mind, he or she actually thinks their shit doesn't stink, and they feel that they're doing you a big favor just walking up to you and starting a conversation.

Don't forget, the customer might not always be right, but they are still the ones that pay your bills. Without them, you wouldn't have a job. So treat them with a little common courtesy and respect! Never try to make a customer feel as if you are in a class above them, or that they are inferior to you.

Some other no, no's, are talking on your cell phone while you are with a customer or leaving them to take a call: glancing down at your wristwatch while you're talking with a client or walking up to a customer with food in your mouth. Come on, where are your manners? I know these situations should be no-brainers, but you would not believe how many times I have seen this happening during the last few months!

Another unforgivable mistake, that many salespeople make, is taking their customers for granted. You do not own a customer, just because they purchased something from you. All relationships must be nurtured to stay solid and keep both parties true to one another.

A husband or wife taking each other for granted is the number one cause of marriage breakups, so you can just imagine how harmful this inconsiderate jester can be when you are trying to build a lasting relationship with a client. Remember, salespeople and customers are a lot like husbands and wives. Customers also need to be romanced and made to feel they are special. If you do not show your customers how much you appreciate them, someone else will be more than happy to show an interest and take them off your hands!

As we weed out bad manners in sales, two unforgivable attitudes stand out in my mind. They are the; "I'm so busy that I don't know what to do" approach. Along with the, "it's almost closing time and I've really got to get out of here," frame of mind. Talk about sales busters, these are monsters!

The idiots that make these mistakes feel that it's imperative to let you know that he, or she, is so busy they really don't have time to wait on you. It's almost like their trying to say, if you want to buy something you better make it quick!

One year after I had made it big in sales I took my wife out to buy her some new clothing and we went to the finest shop in town.

103

I didn't get out of the store I worked for that evening until it was about 5:30. Then I met her at the clothing shop. As we started walking through the isles I told my wife to pick out everything that she liked, and I said, "Don't worry about how much it costs, I've got it covered."

When I first started in sales things were really tight, and she did without, so I could look my best. But I caught on to the selling game quick, and we were able to put away substantial savings that year. Now it was my chance to say thank you for believing in me, and I wanted to do it up right!

After shopping for about twenty-five minutes, we had our arms full of beautiful clothing and one of the snooty sales ladies started to lower the lights. Then she looked at us and announced that the store would be closing in five minutes.

Upon hearing this, I looked at the owner sitting behind a desk in the back of the store and said, "Gee, that's a shame! We were just getting started, and so far we have chosen about 3,800 dollars worth of merchandise we would like to try on and purchase."

With that, the owner sprang to her feet and turned all the lights back on, and we continued our shopping spree. That night, about one hour later, I peeled off 45, 100-dollar bills and paid the lady in cash. Then I said,

"You need to think twice about chasing customers out of your store at the posted closing time, tonight it almost cost you $4,500." She just shook her head and said, "You've got that right!"

Remember, a good salesperson is always ready to help a customer, no matter what time it is!

My motto has always been, any time, any day, anywhere... I'm at your service. I am always ready to make a sale!

At my design studio, Key West Designs, it was a company policy that we would make arrangements to meet any customer at the store after hours, even during the holidays. If you wished to come in and look around the store after you had dinner, or on a Sunday after church, we were more than happy to accommodate you, and that extra service showed up big time in our bank accounts.

Offering customers old-fashioned hospitality with a personal touch was the foundation many of our leading companies were built around when America was first becoming a powerful nation. That sincere desire to help a customer, and make them feel special, still works today if you are willing to give it a try. What's more, you have nothing to lose. All it costs is your time!

It has always been amazing to me how valuable a little common courtesy is. After we stayed late, or reopened the store after hours and showed a customer that kindness, they usually purchased something, and they couldn't wait to tell a friend how enjoyable it was to work with us. These extra courtesies made us stand out from all the other stores in town, and our business kept growing.

Now, we have talked a little bit about some of the worst sales techniques, and why they should be avoided at all cost, so let's shift gears and look at some of the best. You can use these techniques to cozy up to a potential customer. This will put the odds of closing a sale and creating a lifetime client in your favor.

I have always felt that when it comes to making a sale, you have, or you haven't got style! The difference is all in the sales technique you choose, and how you use it!

As for me, I prefer using a slow, gentle approach in selling, even when I ask for a sale. I never get pushy. When you stop and think about it, as soft as a drop of water is it will still bore a hole through a granite boulder over a prolonged period of time. You don't need dynamite to get the job done! Using a slow, easy touch will make the sales experience more personal. This creates a lasting relationship between you and the customer.

I feel most comfortable when a salesperson approaches me with a soft smile, and a gentle greeting that allows me to let them know if I have something in particular that I'm looking for, or whether I'm just taking a little time to do some window-shopping.

If I only want to browse, and the salesperson doesn't come on too strong, I don't mind if he or she stays close by in case I have questions. This gives both of us a chance to get comfortable with each other.

Once I stop, however, and pay attention to one object, more than I have to any other, it's a perfect opportunity for the salesperson to step in, and offer me some points of interest about the item I'm looking at. This is also a chance for the salesperson to start bonding with me. From this moment forward, the two of us will become closer if he or she plays their cards right. I will also be more open and receptive to this salesperson because they showed an interest in me, and seemed to be wise in their ways, and well versed in their product knowledge.

When I taught floor personnel, and interior designers selling techniques at my design studio, Key West Designs, one of the most effective sales methods I introduced them to was the tour guide approach.

To achieve the best results using this style of selling it was imperative that they did their homework to find out everything there was to know about all of the stores merchandise. For my salespeople that meant learning how each piece of furniture was made, where it came from, and how many different ways it could be ordered.

It was important for our salespeople to know what sofas and chairs had eight-way hand-tied coil spring bases, compared to the lesser-expensive no-sag spring units, which were mounted in their frames.

It was also essential to understand how, and why, that difference should concern the customer. Sharing that knowledge made it possible for each salesperson to work as an advocate for the customer by enlightening them when they were considering their options.

Next, the sales personnel needed to know what the insides of the cushions were filled with and what each fabric was made of.

Then to be well-informed salespeople, they also needed to be knowledgeable about how durable each item would be. Which sofa or chair could stand up to heavy wear and tear if used in a customer's family room, and which item should be used in a more formal setting for occasional use only.

After that, when they were showing occasional tables or case goods to a customer, they needed to know how each piece was built. Was each piece built out of solid oak, pecan, teak or cherry? It was also beneficial to know if the tables had dovetailed drawers, and if there were any other interesting details about the craftsmanship that the customer might find intriguing?

Most people love to learn delightful tidbits of information about a piece of furniture they are admiring such as... That beautiful drum table is made of solid oak and has Carpathian Elm Burl wood veneers inlaid in the top.

When a salesperson is able to address a customer with that kind of knowledge, they become a welcome guide, making it easy to accompany the customer on their journey throughout the store.

After that, each of my salespeople and interior designers needed to know who painted every oil painting and watercolor in our studio; along with where each artist was born, where they studied art, and what style or technique they used. They also had to have some knowledge about how each picture was framed. Then they needed to learn as much as they possibly could about every lamp and lampshade in the store, along with a general knowledge about all of the tabletop accessories, etc.

Once they had achieved this, it was time for everyone to go on a field trip. My salespeople needed to look over our competitors operations and check out what they were selling. It was also important to find out how they were running their businesses. After all, you cannot compete with someone, or something that you don't understand!

I taught my sales staff to remember that your competitors have many different ways they can compete with you. These competitive offerings come in such things as; price, service, uniqueness, quality, availability and knowledge. So you must learn what they are selling and find out if they are offering any of the same merchandise or services that you are. Most of all you want to find out how smart they are, and what are their bragging rights.

Once you learn everything you can about your competitors, you'll know how to compete with them in a classy way. Then it's time to start working your magic aggressively!

Never be lulled into a false sense of security by thinking that you do not have any competition. No matter how talented you think you are, someone out there will always try to take you down a notch. The classiest competitor can achieve this feat without seeming rude or distasteful in any way!

As you might imagine, this is just a brief sampling of the depth of knowledge you would need to acquire to utilize the tour guide approach of selling in any type of retail operation. However, the results for anyone willing to exert that much effort are astounding!

This sales strategy accomplishes so many different things in just one brief meeting with a new customer it is a thing of beauty! During your first encounter, you must assume that they will probably want to shop around a little before they commit to buying all their goods from you. That means they are just trying to get a lay of the land on their first outing. When they leave your store, they will be going somewhere else to continue looking and comparing. No matter how many shops they have looked through when they first come into your store, you would be safe in guessing they probably have not found a place with such knowledgeable salespeople as yours. However, since you used the tour-guide sales approach, you have made these potential customers a ticking time bomb for any other store they might visit.

It has been said, a little knowledge is a dangerous thing, and you have utilized your time with these potential new customers to enlighten them with enough bits and pieces of product knowledge to drive the next salesperson out of their mind.

Now, every new salesperson that they meet is going to be inundated with questions about their merchandise, and when they stumble and fumble around, unable to answer all their questions, the customer is going to be thinking about how knowledgeable you were. After a day of that, they will make a beeline back to your store and ask for you by name!

You always want to remember, knowledge is power in sales! Once you learn as much as you can, share that knowledge with everyone you meet. Every time you share your knowledge with someone, you're planting a seed. Just like Johnny Apple Seed realized, some of those seeds are bound to grow. So plant a seed in a fertile mind and grow a sale! Each time you do, you will continue to build a loyal following and those customers will spread the word to their family and friends. The business that comes in from referrals alone will double your income and start you well on your way to success, just like it worked for me.

William S. Crenshaw

CHAPTER 7
CREATE A DESIRE

As you travel on your journey through life working as a salesperson, every potential client or customer that you come across will have needs, wants, and uncharted dreams. Everyone can find their basic needs or necessities on their own. However, finding the stuff that dreams are made of will not be so easy.

Although most people recognize what they like when they hear it, or see it unveiled for the very first time, the vast majority of those in search of their dreams will never find them without a guide. That will give you an opportunity to assist them.

Clients who hire you to perform a service, or customers who hope you will lead them to a secret stash of mesmerizing merchandise, have a hard time describing their hopes, dreams, and desires. Deep down inside they are hoping you will help them make a significant discovery, and sweep them off their feet.

115

They figure you will achieve this by introducing them to an offering so inspiring, or merchandise so incredible, that it will blow their minds. But when it comes to helping you figure out what they are searching for, any assistance they might offer can be quite confusing, to say the least. This leaves the job of translating descriptions and navigating your way through each client's list of desires up to you.

A talented salesperson learns how to read between the lines and will make it fun for every customer to spend their money. They achieve this by showing creativity and by dazzling each new buyer with their ability to create a desire, for the goods or merchandise they show them.

Since most people don't know where to search for their dreams, and have a hard time describing them, they feel uncertain where to begin. Because of their lack of imagination, many of them feel they will never find their hearts desire, so they wind up settling for something. Sad to say, what they settle for is usually far less than what they would have chosen, or could have had, if that magic "something" sounded off, or appeared in front of them before they made that fateful decision.

To make sure that doesn't happen to your clients you must prepare for each encounter by creating a

SELL IT! There's A Job For Everyone

series of introductory offerings that you can use to break the ice and inspire them. These offerings need to be exciting enough to show your potential clients that you have the ability to help make their dreams come true.

In order to land a contract for any service, it's a good idea to lead into your sales pitch with examples. These offerings need to be exciting enough to open their minds to what you have. Once your clients understand what's in store for them, they will usually look forward to coming along for the ride.

The best service offerings usually come in the form of guidance, planning, or plans, shared knowledge, insight, introductions, and in many cases, a personal hands-on service, which you might offer to help them get the job done. Sometimes showing attractive samples of previous service offerings, which you have already completed, will ease the clients mind and help you close the sale... especially if those projects were exciting and successful.

Another sure-fire addition to any sales pitch is showing your clients how the offering you're proposing will benefit them. There's not a person alive who doesn't hope to profit in some way from every transaction they make.

When I worked as a designer, one of the services I offered was landscape design. Through the years, many of the landscape companies in my area offered their clients free design services if they purchased plants and hired them to do the installation. Because of that cutthroat way of doing business, many of the landscape architects gave up and moved, but I decided to fight back.

I knew that I had the ability to create a desire with my artwork, and recapture a share of the market in design services. I also knew if I played my cards right, other landscape contractors would be willing to pay me a commission for selling each project and recommending their services to install the jobs I designed. In order to compete from a position of strength, I needed inside knowledge as to how my competitors were handling their projects.

When I decided to make my move, the first thing I did was contact some of the customers who had used the services of these other landscape companies. Then I ask them if they would be kind enough to show me their plans and tell me how they felt about the contractors work. I told them, I was considering using these companies to install my projects, so I needed some honest referrals.

Some said no, but most of the people I asked said sure, why not. During those meetings, not only did I get a chance to see what all of the other landscape contractor's designs and blueprints looked like, I was also able to learn what their sales pitches were and find the openings I needed.

Most of the other contractor's plans were vague, and they lacked any real art ability. Since their plans were free, these contractors didn't put any effort at all in creating a desire for what the project could look like. They were only interested in finding a way to grab the sugar and run.

This was a sad way to do business, and it seemed to leave some of their customers with a bad taste in their mouths. Many of them had unfulfilled dreams of what they hoped to wind up with when the job was done. The magic was definitely missing!

As I talked to these homeowners, I could see how an entire business could be built just following the landscapers around and creating a desire for what they had left out of the work they had performed. By offering something for nothing, to eliminate the competition, they had chased off many designers, but their laziness and lack of talent had left me the opportunity of a lifetime. After witnessing that, I realized I would never run out of satisfied customers!

119

Here, once again, a simple field trip gave me insider's knowledge to find out exactly what I needed to know to compete.

When it comes to selling retail merchandise, the same thing holds true. Each new customer is hoping to be wowed, and surprised by the displays you have set up to tempt them with, and you better not let them down.

Remember, you only get one chance to make a good first impression, so don't get lazy and blow it! Always make an effort to dazzle each new customer and create a desire for the products you're selling.

People usually learn how to shop by searching for things they need. Once they have taken care of their basic needs, they start spending more time thinking about their wants. Then they begin window-shopping. However, most customers have no idea what will astound them. The job of stimulating that thought process is up to you!

The trick to becoming an exceptional salesperson is learning how to romance each customer with visions of merchandise that will forever haunt them. That is the "art" of creating a desire. When you master that ability there will be no end to the amount of merchandise, or services, you will be able to sell.

No matter who you are, or what you're selling, you will have better luck landing the sale if you learn how to create a desire for your services and products.

Whether you're selling, Stocks, bonds, furniture, accessories, fine jewelry, automobiles, plastic surgery, clothing, furs, flooring, lighting fixtures, real estate, fine art, produce, insurance, tools, hardware, plumbing supplies, fine china, Persian rugs, saddles and western wear, trucks, tractors, trailers, airplanes, ski boats, yachts or the trip of a lifetime, everything sells better when it's presented in a most-desirable way.

Just look at what Bass Masters did with their sales outlets. Who would have ever thought that buying fishing gear could be so much fun!

When the shopping experience is fun for your customers, it's more profitable for you.

Throughout history less-talented storeowners and salespeople, have tried to create a desire for their goods by offering the lowest price in town. This mindset usually comes from a lack of knowledge. These storeowners and their sales staff have no idea what most customers are willing to spend if they are properly romanced. By focusing on selling the lowest price items they can find, and spending their life trying to undercut everyone around them, they will never realize what incredible things there are to sell, and how profitable selling can be. This type of merchandising will also make it impossible for their sales staff to find out how much they could have earned as a top-notch salespeople.

If you hope to discover how successful you can be, you must open your heart and mind to the possibilities around you, and reach for the stars. Remember, not everyone in the world is a cheapskate.

Most people are hoping to discover brave new merchants and knowledgeable salespeople that will give them an opportunity to better themselves. Every time you sell-up in quality, you are helping your customers elevate themselves to a better place in life.

You should also remember that it's not up to you to make judgment calls pertaining to what a customer can or cannot afford to spend.

It's a fact that some of the most expensive items you will ever sell, will be purchased by customers you thought couldn't afford them. That's why they created revolving charge accounts. So don't be fooled into thinking anything is too expensive for the people in your area to purchase.

It would probably surprise you to learn how much money is being taken out of town and spent on those nicer items, and then brought back home, right under your nose. When it comes to sales, remember... no guts, no glory!

I hope you never get caught up in this buy-now-and-pay-later vicious circle. However, credit accounts are a fundamental part of the sales game. Your job is not saving people from themselves its moving merchandise!

If you decide to go for the gusto in life and reach for the stars as I did, you will need to learn how to create a desire in the minds of your potential customers for the finer things in life. Then you have to be willing to show them how to get there.

Merchandising, display and presentation have always been the three main ingredients in creating a desire and capturing the minds of customers everywhere. Once you've caught the customer's attention, and opened their minds to the possibilities surrounding them, you will have an opportunity to share your knowledge and inspire them by placing each one of them in the dream you're pitching. Now the shopping experience of a lifetime will be theirs. You always want to make sure the person you're working with has an enjoyable time spending their money!

If you do your job right, the sales pitch, display, or presentation you make, will set their minds adrift in a sea of inspiration.

Next, it's also essential to teach new clients, or customers, how many different ways they can buy your services or products. Don't forget, this might be a new experience for them. So help them learn how to do it right. Once they learn that there is more than one way to achieve their desired goal they will have a chance to discover a plan that will work for them and your sales will grow. The more you help each new client, or customer, the more it will benefit you.

In the furniture business, and world of interior design, I was taught how to look ahead and consider different scenarios that pertained to selling high-end products. Because the merchandise we sold was so expensive, the average customer might not be able to afford a whole house full of furniture at one time. However, if we taught our customers why wealthy people purchase items the way they do, they could learn how to buy merchandise that would be in style forever and they could buy it one piece at a time.

Most well educated people are taught to appreciate classical styles of home furnishings and accessories, and wealthy customers usually hire interior designers to help them decorate their homes and offices. Therefore, the art of mixing and matching merchandise is second nature to them. This style of decorating is called eclectic.

Because of the timeless beauty that these goods possess, a customer can add to their collection forever and never wind up with something that is out dated, or out of style. Quite the contrary, most of their furniture and accessories will become tomorrow's priceless antiques.

Using this sales technique is a win-win strategy for everyone concerned! You will make a friend for life out of your potential new clients and sales customers by educating them, and they will keep coming back to your business year after year.

In the mid-1980s, I was hired to design a beautiful new jewelry store for a wealthy jeweler in Central California, and he was an artist in every way. What made him so successful, however, was his ability to warm up to his customers making each one feel that they were the most important people in the world. His persona was a big part of his ability to create a desire.

In the beginning, he achieved this feat by approaching each client with style and grace. His merchandise was exquisite, to say the least. After he had become successful, and had made a reputation for carrying the valley's finest merchandise, he decided to take the art of selling jewelry to the next level. To achieve this goal he knew that he had to create a new environment.

125

After he had hired me, my first job as a designer was to observe his store, customers, and the people who worked there.

Then I was to create a brand new setting for them to display their merchandise in and boost their sales.

As I observed his day-to-day operations, I couldn't help but notice how uncomfortable many of his customers were, bending over the glass counters, to view his finest rings and necklaces. I also noticed how awkward it was for him, and his salesclerks, to pace back and forth behind the counter getting from one piece of jewelry to the next.

A major part of the owner's warmth and charisma came from his one on one approach with his customers. So anything I could do to enhance that experience and make his customers feel more comfortable should increase his sales.

Once I thought about this for a while, an interesting idea came to me. He was truly the star of this operation and his customers doted on him, so why not make him the center of attraction.

To achieve that goal and create a desire for his finest merchandise I designed an incredible sitting area in the center of the store, which I placed on an elevated platform. Then I had a custom cabinetmaker build a huge octagonal showcase, shaped like a giant coffee table, for the center of the sitting area.

The coffee table was designed to look like the world's largest jewelry box, and the sides all had keyed openings unlocking two-foot sections of glass. This allowed the owner to spin the showcase around in front of his customers and pull out an unbelievable piece of jewelry without ever standing up, or leaving their side. The pedestal base for this showpiece was entirely hand-carved, and the top was a combination of glass and handmade brass fittings. The table itself was so beautiful that it literally took your breath away when it was empty, so you can imagine how impressive it was when he filled it with his finest jewelry.

Next, I set the beautiful table on a large round hand-knotted Persian rug. Then I surrounded the showcase with two diamond-tufted, crescent shaped sofas, in burgundy velvet. I then topped off the setting with an oversized three-tier crystal chandelier.

The chandelier hung from a canopy in the middle of a hand-carved floral ceiling, patterned after a 17th Century French floral painting that I used in the foyer.

The overall color scheme for the shop was burgundy, royal blue and hunter green with dove-grey and coral backdrops. This created a contrast between the deep, rich colors and the beautiful jewels, which made every piece of jewelry seem to leap out of the cabinets in front of your eyes.

To overcome the awkward feeling of having to bend way over to see the merchandise that was displayed in the other upright showcases, I had a glass man build the standing displays with stair-stepped glass shelving. This made every piece of jewelry visible at a glance, and the right lighting effects did the rest.

To finish off the stores décor I located some unbelievable photographs of many of the world's most valuable pieces of jewelry and had them enlarged, matted, and framed. Then I used the pictures to dress the interior walls.

All of the fabrication of the cabinets, the huge jewel box coffee table and the hand-carved woodwork, was created in a warehouse.

The framing, electrical wiring, painting, carpet and installation of all the key elements, was completed with the store only being shut down for two weeks. The grand opening was an enormous success.

This jeweler truly understood the importance of creating a desire.

The new customers that were drawn to the remodeled store all seemed to be looking for more expensive items, and this drastically changed the amount of profit he made on every new sale. By stirring the imagination of his old and new customers and creating a desire to see his beautiful new showroom, he doubled his profits without having to move into a larger store.

Nothing revs up sales like creating a desire! I've seen this sales technique build up to a fever pitch in almost every industry.

Through the years, I've watched people buy everything a company had in stock, of a certain make or model of merchandise, because of the desire created by the perfect display or advertising campaign. Then, when the item sold out, customers would sign up on a waiting list so that they would be the first ones in line to purchase the next available item that came off the assembly line.

This took place with Chrysler's first minivan and their PT Cruiser. In most of these incidents, the car lots were even able to charge more than the suggested retail price because of the demand. This was all accomplished by creating a desire, for the merchandise they hoped to sell.

In my design studio, Key West Designs, the perfect window display would often be the reason for an entire boxcar of merchandise selling out within a week. Then customers would make regular visits to our showroom to see our newest displays because we had mastered the art of creating a desire.

What's more, we were able to sell our merchandise for the full retail price without having to mark it down, like other retailers did, and our customers returned year after year. Price was not the driving force that brought customers to our store, desire was!

Creating a desire really does work, and while sales will always be necessary to close out discontinued merchandise and to make way for new items, you should beware of developing a reputation for being a discount store. That's a hard reputation to shake!

Most of your finest retail establishments limit their sales to two full-blown closeout sales per year, which are connected to their buying trips. They also advertise that fact to let their customers know that there is a legitimate reason for having these sales. Then, they create other special events spread evenly throughout the year to keep a steady flow of foot traffic coming into the store.

You don't have to give something away to draw a crowd. Just use a little creativity. There are millions of ways to create a desire!

William S. Crenshaw

CHAPTER 8
THE PERFECT PAPER TRAIL

Becoming a top-notch salesperson takes more than just the ability to tell a mesmerizing story and create a desire, you must also have the skills to write a proper sales contract and keep your business affairs in order.

It's funny, but no one in business likes to think, or talk about paperwork, and until now, all we've talked about is the art of making a sale. But I would be letting you down if I didn't start your sales career off in the right direction.

You see there are right ways and wrong ways to do just about everything, and most beginners in sales have no idea how important paperwork can be.

Every successful businessperson will tell you one of the most crucial things in business is your paperwork. Without utilizing the proper paperwork, there is no end to the amount of chaos you might go

William S. Crenshaw

through, and no one needs that kind of confusion or heartache. You must learn the importance of paperwork to become successful, no matter whether you are in retail sales, a self-employed salesperson, or you are currently working as an account executive for a major Corporation. Simply put paperwork levels the playing field where you do business. Good paperwork can keep you safe from customers who change their mind in the middle of a project, or unscrupulous business people who are always looking for the opportunity to take advantage of a trusting soul.

The proper documents will also outline every service you are obligated to perform and spell out exactly what you have agreed to provide. Always remember, a sales pitch is worthless until it's been reduced to writing, and no sale is complete until a perfectly executed sales-contract is agreed to then signed and dated by both parties.

The perfect sales contract should always show the company's full name and street address, not just a PO BOX. It should also list the full name of the contact person who is signing the contract, along with the company's area code, phone number, and their fax number when possible.

The more information you can obtain and write down on a contract the better it is for you. All of this information could be invaluable while working through the completion of the project and collecting the final payment once the job is done.

Through experience, I have also learned that it is a smart idea to make sure the person, or company you are doing business with, has an equal investment in whatever you are involved in together. When the other party does not have a monetary investment in the sale or project, they can change their mind and simply walk away at any time. However, when the customer places a nonrefundable deposit of 50% down, you both have an equal stake in the outcome.

It's surprising how much more cooperative the second party is when they have the same amount to gain or lose, as you.

At my company, a sales contract must always be accompanied by a deposit check of half the contract price. Once the contract is signed, and the deposit check clears the bank, all work begins.

In one of Kenny Rogers' most popular songs titled The Gambler, he sings… every hand's a winner and every hand's a loser, and nothing could be closer to the truth when it comes to a sale.

Almost all sales start out as exciting moments, filled with high expectations in both the salespersons mind and that of the customer. However, there are a

135

million reasons why that excitement can fade and turn into anger or distrust, and when that takes place the project can end up in a dispute.

Once a disagreement takes place, he said, or she said statements are worthless in court. At that time, the only thing that will give an accurate accounting of what has been going on is the paper trail that is left behind.

Most judges will tell you there are always three sides to every story, theirs, yours, and the truth!

When any transaction winds up making it's way into the court system, all of the contracts you have signed and any other signed documents will become the deciding factors as to who will prevail.

Great salespeople have always protected themselves by getting something signed every chance they get! Most of them have learned this lesson the hard way, and have come to realize that paperwork is their friend.

It's unbelievable how many times people have changed their mind in every business I've been a part of. However, thanks to the proper paperwork to back up what took place, I have always been on the winning side. Remember, signed documents keep things straight. Contracts, and signed paperwork protect all parties involved in any transaction, so it's a win-win situation all the way around.

There are many different types of documents that will become an indispensable part of your life if you're involved in sales, and you should take an interest in all of them. As I told you before, knowledge is power in sales. So never shy away from learning everything you can about any paperwork that can help you in your chosen field.

If a contract, or any other document you are forced to read, or prepare, is difficult for you to understand, you should always seek legal advice from an attorney before you, or anyone else, signs it.

It is also necessary to know not only your rights, but also the rights of your customers, under the law. This way you can be certain that the paperwork you have prepared will stand up in court if the need arises.

To make sure that you always have the right paperwork for every situation, you should begin by thinking through all the scenarios that might take place in your day-to-day sales routines.

Whatever it is that you intend to sell; you will most certainly need to start with a standard sales contract. If you decide to build a contract from scratch it would be a good idea to go online and find a generic sales contract that pertains to your business, then tweak it to meet your needs.

Remember however, a generic sales contract that has not been customized is an accident waiting to take place. Every different business has its own specific needs when it comes to addressing legal matters, and most people will not find out what theirs are until they're in court. So do yourself a favor and rework the contract before you use it!

Some of the key elements you should have in any contract are the phrases: 'Your contract with (you or your company's name here), is an integrated contract; no prior or contemporaneous representations, promises, offers, or counteroffers not expressly set forth in this writing have any legal force or effect.'

The statement above has made it clear that you are only agreeing to exactly what is written in the contract. Now the other party cannot say you promised them something else verbally, or that you misled them in any way.

Next, you should state in your contract that you are not agreeing to any specific deadlines, or delivery times, unless they have been specified in writing.

You should also state that you are not offering or implying any warranties, or guarantees of any kind, and note that any changes to this contract must be made in writing then signed, and dated, by both parties.

If you are selling merchandise, make sure to state that all merchandise is sold F.O.B. (the name of your city). Then spell out the fact that the customer will be responsible for any delivery charges outside of your designated area. Also, mention any other expenses that the customer is expected to pay for, such as travel, lodging, and meals, if this connects with your services.

After that, clearly state that if any legal action is required to enforce their legal obligation to you, or your company, the customer will be responsible for all collection costs including a reasonable attorney's fee.

Lastly spell out in the body text of your contract, regardless of where the contract is entered into, and the work performed, you are both agreeing to have your case tried in (the courts of your jurisdiction) in case you end up going to court.

NOTE: Because I am not an attorney I cannot, and am not giving you legal advice. I am simply suggesting that you consider these terms for use in your documents. It is always smart to have an attorney check the final layout of your contract before you have it printed and put it into use.

Once you have a solid sales contract ready to go, it's also necessary to prepare a receiving copy. You should never deliver anything, or let anyone pick anything up without having them sign for it, even if they pay you with cash! Remember, a customer can smile, and pay you today... then sue you tomorrow, and the only thing that will set things straight will be your contract and signed receiving copy.

Again, it is essential that the receiving copy state that the person signing it is receiving everything they ordered in full. It should also state that they are 100% happy with the merchandise, and are accepting everything **AS IS**. This document also needs to be signed and dated, as well.

If you are working for a business that already has a sales contract, study theirs. You should memorize, or at least familiarize yourself with the standard clauses in the contract and make sure you don't vary from what the contract spells out.

If, for example, the contract clearly states that no merchandise will be ordered, or work preformed, until a deposit is placed for one-half of the contract sales price, then follow that guideline.

As a graphic designer, I am constantly hit on by new customers and asked for a sneak preview of what their design might look like if they hire me. They are hoping to see something before they commit, sign a contract and place their deposit. But my answer is always no! At that point, I am bargaining from a position of strength, so why would I want to weaken my position.

If you are weak, or needy, people will take advantage of you so stand your ground! No matter how large or small a contract is I never begin work on any project until a contract is signed and a deposit is placed.

If the customer is nervous about the quality of my work, or whether they will be happy with the finished product, I have a number of samples constantly on hand, to prove how talented I am. Showing off letters of recommendation and incredible photos of past design projects always seals the deal.

If the contract also clearly states no changes to the contract will be valid unless the change is made in writing and has been signed by an authorized person from both parties, then do not make changes to your work in any way unless the requested changes have been agreed to in writing, and signed by both parties.

Your contract is like a bodyguard, and it can't protect you unless you stand behind it and believe in it.

Once you change the rules by doing something different than the contract states, you set a precedent, and you could live to regret it. This might sound like an inconvenience, but it can mean the difference between being paid and having a happy customer at the end of the project, or being sued and losing your profit when the job is done. The contract must be followed to the letter if it is going to protect both of you!

When I worked as a designer in the building trades, I designed custom homes, office buildings, and restaurants. During that time, I was often asked by the owners of these projects to work as their project manager. My job was to see that the project turned out the way I envisioned it and to make sure the sub contractors stayed within the budget that was agreed to.

At that time, one of my closest friends was a building contractor, and he was constantly complaining about how many times he had been screwed out of final payments for change orders.

One day I asked him if I could see one of his standard change order documents and he just looked at me and shrugged his shoulders. "I don't have a standard change order document", he said. With that, I said, "Don't you think it's about time you got your paperwork in order? How much money do you have to lose before you change the way you do business?"

When my clients hired me to oversee their building project, no matter who asked for additional work, I always got a quote in writing for any changes. I also made sure that no additional work was preformed until I showed the quote to my client first, then had it approved, and signed for on a change order form.

Because of my ironclad policies and procedures, none of the subcontractors on any of my projects was ever cheated out of their money. My clients were also happy because no one could take advantage of them.

I learned early on that all human beings have convenient memories, and I include myself in that category. Most of us are so spread out, over the day-to-day struggle of running our lives that we can lose track of things. Being inundated with so many activities we would swear we said, or did not say, something weeks or months ago, when, in fact, the opposite was true. But a signed piece of paper quickly refreshes our memory, and everyone is happy.

Having paperwork signed for everything imaginable might seem like an inconvenience, but, in fact, it's a short cut to sanity.

Other documents that come in handy are work-in-progress forms that show how a project is going. This form makes everything clear, and shows that the customer is being kept in the loop. A form such as this can also be invaluable for a variety of projects in different industries, not just construction.

Another handy form is the final walk-through document. This signoff sheet confirms that all of the contracted work is complete. Or, it spells out exactly what it will take to finish the project. This document cuts the ring down to size if a project is dragging on, and gives both parties a chance to see where the finish line is.

Once again, this form can be used in a wide range of different occupations.

In other businesses like the printing industry, original contracts need to spell out exactly what a customer is purchasing. It should include what the product is, the number of copies being purchased and how many colors of ink will be used to print the project. It should also specify the size the finished items will be, and what special coatings will be used on the cover, if it is a book, folder, or poster. Next it should state the cost for the overall layout, design and all pre-press work.

Once the design and layouts are complete for a project, it's time to have it inspected by the client. Then it must be approved, and signed off to go to print. This requires the proper paperwork just like the necessary documents for any other type of business.

A sign-off document specifies that everyone has done their best to locate and correct all mistakes in the layouts, to the best of their ability. However, mistakes do happen. Therefore, it is (the customer's) responsibility to review the layouts carefully, and look for any errors or omissions. Then sign, and date, in the blank below. In this document, you should state that (you or your company) would not be responsible for any errors or mistakes after printing takes place.

Neither a customer, nor a printing company wants to eat a printing job if an error is made in spelling. But no one is perfect. In fact, there have even been misspelled words found in Webster's Dictionary, and that is the bible when it comes to spelling. So anyone can make a mistake. But thanks to the perfect sign-off document, everyone can have their chance to discover whatever mistakes have been made before the piece goes to print, and the printer can have peace of mind.

No matter what you sell, you will not last long and stay profitable, without using the proper paperwork to write up your sales and keep and your business safe. This is also true when it comes to reaching out and romancing a customer by mail.

A proposal is another valuable document that most salespeople will use at one time or another throughout their careers, and this document is always custom made. This means no two proposals are ever the same. But do not let that fool you! Though no two documents are ever written exactly the same, there are certain things that you do not want to leave out of a well-written proposal.

145

Since there are certain elements that you can't afford to leave out of this document, it's wise to create a master form that you always work from. This paperwork will ensure your success when you draft your next proposal.

In this document, you will usually reach out to someone that you wish to do business with, and make the pitch of a lifetime. If you prepare it right, the result could be worth a fortune to you. However, if you make it too long and drawn out, the person you are hoping to romance might not take the time to read it at all.

A proposal is probably one of the most difficult documents to prepare properly, but it will be invaluable to you once you have learned how to master it. Some authors have said writing the perfect proposal is harder than writing a book.

Through the years, my clients have used proposals to reach out to sponsors, locate start up capital, and find openings to market a wide range of products. During this time, I have had a front row seat, as I watched my own company's sales representatives use proposals to land some of our largest sales.

The best proposals closely resembled the type of letter a writer would prepare to send off when they are searching for an agent, or book publisher. They call them query letters. These letters can make, or break, a writers chance to get their foot in the door, and have their work published.

Most publishing companies and agents have created some narrow guidelines in order to streamline the process of weeding out worthwhile documents to read. This only makes sense when you think about how many letters and proposals they receive in the mail each day.

When you write a proposal, you should take for granted that the person you are addressing is extremely busy, so getting junk mail is not a thrill. I know you don't consider your proposal junk mail, but if you received a plain brown envelope in the mail containing a lackluster letter that was written by a person you have never heard of, what would you call it? This is how most people present themselves, and you have to admit it is not very romantic.

To hedge your bet, you might think of making the proposal visually mind-blowing, and then keep the information inside short and to the point. To achieve that goal you need to remember how to create a desire, and light a fire in the imagination of your potential customers.

By creating beautiful business cards, letterhead, and envelopes, you will always have the perfect paperwork you need to reach out and touch someone.

147

Then you should create an incredible presentation folder to use for packaging these materials.

The brochures and other advertising materials you invest in should never look homemade. Using homemade material to introduce yourself to a potential customer makes you look like you are either going through hard times, or just have poor taste. Either way, you should never embarrass yourself like that.

Instead of trying to create your own brochures, to save money, consider how much the perfect piece of advertising material will make you if it helps you land a sale. So be courageous and show some class. Then step up to the plate and knock it out of the park.

To sum it all up your paperwork is, and always will be, what you will use for the beginning, middle, and end of every transaction you make.

William S. Crenshaw

CHAPTER 9
NEVER LET ANYONE STAND IN YOUR WAY

Successful entrepreneurs and salespeople alike realize there's money to be made from the moment an idea is conceived. After that, one chance to sell the idea turns into ten; ten chances turn into twenty and the sales opportunities continue to multiply as the idea floats downstream. If you follow an idea from its original conception to the manufacturing of a product, then all the way to the end user, you will be amazed how many times a single thought, or product, must be studied, pitched, and sold, to become a reality. Most exciting of all is the fact that each time you see someone's eyes light up with a new idea; it just might be the opportunity you've been looking for to make your fortune in sales.

To get some idea of just how many sales opportunities exist each year, you should begin by multiplying every saleable concept in the world by three.

151

First, as every new idea floats downstream, the concept and its marketability are presented to an investor, banker, or money person. This sales pitch is made to raise enough work capital to produce the product, and that's just the beginning.

Second, after each item is produced, the finished product must be dressed up and properly packaged. Then it's presented or sold to the wholesale market.

This usually involves building a promotional campaign to sell the item to the retail storeowners at shows, conventions, and merchandise marts.

Third, the retailer buys the item for a wholesale price with the intention of selling it to the public, or end user, for a suggested retail price. Then a whole new series of sales efforts begin.

Next, in order to sell the product to the public, both the manufacturer, and the retailer, will launch advertising campaigns to reach out to the widest possible consumer base. But the sales pitches and advertising campaigns don't end there.

To make sure each of these groups did not miss out on an opportunity to make every possible sale, they will start a series of advertising campaigns aimed at selling the sellers. This means even the middlemen, and women, working for retail operations are now being inundated with sales pitches.

As the advertising campaigns start to work, word of mouth spreads and enthusiastic salespeople reach out from one town to another. Now the product they're pitching has an opportunity to become the next must-have item, and this strategy can often create a selling frenzy. After that, literally thousands of sales efforts will be made to keep the product moving forward to its final destination.

By this time, you can imagine how many sales pitches have been made just to sell this one item, probably at least a gazillion! That's why I believe the field of sales offers a job for everyone.

Once I realized how money flows downstream, and saw the sales opportunities each new idea creates, I knew how bright my future was going to be. Now I could see the open doorway leading to my destiny. I guess that's what drew me into the world of advertising sales. To me this was the ultimate sales job, and when it came to prospects, there was no end in sight.

My first full time job in sales was working in a furniture store when I was in my late teens, and outside sales representatives seemed like the luckiest people on the planet.

Every week a different salesperson, showed up at our store riding in a shiny new car, and they would introduce my boss to an exciting new line of furniture, lamps, and accessories.

Because of my outstanding sales record, the owner would invite me to sit in on these get-togethers in order to hear my views before he purchased any new merchandise.

Attending these impromptu meetings was both entertaining and educational to me, as well. Not only was I able to see the latest in new merchandise, but I also got to watch, and listen to, another unique sales pitch being made by a consummate professional. When it came to class and style, these sales people were in a league of their own.

I guess what impressed me the most about one rep in particular; however, was the depth of his knowledge, and how he was able to stretch a sale.

Not only did this salesman get your heart racing before he wrote up an order, but he continued after the sale was closed by helping you figure out the best way to move the merchandise you had purchased. You see, he realized once everything you purchased was sold, you would need to reorder. By investing a little more time with each customer, while he was at their store, the Henredon rep was able to turn an opening sale into two, three, or four, additional sales, and the storeowner loved him for it!

One day, out of curiosity, I sat down with my favorite salesman and asked him to share some of his knowledge with me. I told him that I couldn't stop thinking about the way he approached each sale. I was especially interested to learn how he was trained to think through a sale. His answers were quite fascinating, to say the least.

"In the beginning", he said, "I was surprised to learn that Henredon spent more time worrying about helping retail storeowners move their merchandise, than they spent thinking of selling their own. Henredon knew the key to ultimate profitability was getting their furniture into people's homes not making quick sales to retail storeowners, and leaving them to fend for themselves. This meant each representative was urged to learn everything they could about retail sales. Then they were instructed to follow up on every sale they made by assisting the storeowner in any way possible to help them move that merchandise."

He then continued by saying, "My boss told me not to celebrate a singular sale. Instead, I was encouraged to put all of my efforts in creating repeat business. An opening sales order wasn't a victory, but an opportunity for bigger things to come."

By heeding this philosophy, he had become their number one sales rep. Now every time a customer placed an order they were getting much more than they had bargained for. Before the ink had dried on the paper the order was written on, he was contemplating the best possible combination of goods that could be displayed together to draw attention to the items he had just sold.

Then he would pull out some incredible line art for newspaper ads, featuring the same Henredon furniture, and tell the owner that Henredon would help him pay for the cost of running the ads, if he would place them in the newspaper.

He said, "Henredon attributed much of their success to assuming that a typical storeowner could not build the most attractive newspaper ads and write the best copy to lure customers into their store. So Henredon took it upon themselves to hire the finest talent available and create the ads for them." He went on to say, " Henredon also realized many of the retail storeowners might be a little cheap when it came to running the ads, even if they got the ad slicks free, so they started offering them co-op advertising rates to get the ads in the newspaper. This paid off big time through the years. By going this extra distance, Henredon was able to avoid a logjam and keep their merchandise flowing downstream straight into the customers homes and offices. The rest is history!"

Then he looked at me and said, "Never let someone else's unwillingness to do the right thing, get in the way of your success. Do whatever needs to be done, even if you have to figure out a way to pay for it, yourself. You'll be rewarded handsomely for your courage and wisdom in the end."

That conversation guided me in the right direction throughout my career, and it played a vital role in helping me become an exceptional salesman. From that moment on, I realized there is a lot more to becoming successful in the field of sales than just buying and selling goods. It is vital that each salesperson learns everything about moving a product downstream to its final destination. Then the process can begin again.

It takes a steady flow of orders, and sales, continuously moving in a full circle to create the perfect business. This harmony makes buying and selling a profitable, and enjoyable, experience for everyone concerned.

From that time on, I never looked at a singular sale as something to celebrate. Instead, I began thinking of each first sale as an opening for other sales to come.

When a company I was working for offered me top quality sales aides, I utilized them to help me do my job. However, if they were tight-fisted with their money, and wouldn't spend what it took to create the things I needed to help me achieve my desired goals, I created my own. And just as my friend said, I always profited from investing in myself.

As I think back through 50 years of working in sales, and all of the different business owners I have known, it is unreal how many of them stood in the way of their own success by being scared, or greedy, when it came to spending their own money to promote a sale. But I never made that crucial mistake. I took that lesson to heart.

Two other things I learned from that gentleman was, how important it is to get your foot in the door, and once you get inside you want to work the room for everything its worth.

I was also impressed by his vim and vigor. He didn't have a lazy bone in his body, and he wasn't one to waste time. Instead of sitting in the showroom waiting for the phone to ring, or hoping a customer would drop by, he hit the road and went to every store in his territory. By making a habit of visiting his customer's shops in person, he was able to form a closer bond with each of the owners, and their sales staff. He also wanted to see, first hand, what other merchandise each store was carrying, and how they displayed their goods. While he was at each store, he also took time to make sure their catalog and swatches were kept up-to-date. After all, it wouldn't be beneficial for his business if a stores salesman, or interior designer, special ordered a custom sofa or credenza from the catalog, only to find out a week later that those items had been discontinued. This combination of traits is what made this sales rep special. A lesser quality salesperson, who might be a little lazy and unwilling to spend so much time on the road, would simply pass the task of updating samples, swatches, and price lists to the stores salespeople and hope for the best. But this guy was all business and he controlled his own destiny by never shifting that responsibility!

Some salespeople try their best to make every sale from inside their store. These people literally hate to go out on calls. But the real money to be made is found hidden away in every home and business. These areas represent your potential customer's comfort zones. This is where they are the most likely to let their hair down and open up to your proposals and recommendations.

Once you get an invitation to come inside one of these special places, the entire sales game changes in your favor.

William S. Crenshaw

Whether it's an item you're selling or an idea, you will have better luck landing the sale if you make the customer comfortable and get them to take part in your sales pitch.

After I talked to the Henredon sales rep, and watched him work, I decided to try some of his methods when I got the chance to go out on my own appointments.

Back then, most of our outside sales calls were initiated by meeting someone new in the furniture store. After walking them through the showroom and answering their questions, you had an opportunity to offer your decorating services in their home where you could help them with their overall design needs.

When I began venturing out on my first appointments, I realized it was a privilege to be invited into someone's home, so I always showed them the utmost respect. I did this by getting to know them, and learning how they lived and used each of the rooms in their house before I presumed to make any recommendations.

Then, I asked how many people lived in the house, and what their ages were. By asking these questions, I was able to gain a better perspective of what their overall needs would be. First, we needed to focus on function, then on beauty.

SELL IT! There's A Job For Everyone

Next, I would ask the homeowner to show me some of their most prized possessions. Things like heirlooms that were passed down through the family, or items that the husband and wife had been collecting since they began their lives together. I also asked if there were any pieces of furniture or accessories that they would never want to part with, and last, but not least, what their favorite colors were. After that, I was ready to begin the design project.

Now, just like the Henredon sales rep, I had gotten my foot in the door and obtained enough personal information to make sound judgment calls, when it came to recommendations. I was also ready to do more than just sell furniture and accessories to the customer. From this time on, I could make buying and selling a more personal experience.

With each new job, my talent grew and referral projects soon started coming my way. By this time, I had some intriguing stories to tell, and I realized how handy before and after pictures would be when it came to helping me close a sale.

One day, with that in mind, I approached my boss and told him about my idea. Since I was the stores top salesperson I was hoping he would see the wisdom of purchasing some high quality photography and watching it pay off in plus sales, but all he could think about was how much money it would cost. When I had completed making my sales pitch, he just looked at me and said, "We've got a Polaroid camera under the counter, why don't you use that to take your pictures? It would be way too expensive to hire a professional photographer to shoot the kind of shots you're talking about."

Opportunity was knocking on his door, but he couldn't hear it. It was clear he didn't get it, or he was too cheap to spend the money it would take to chase a dream. But I remembered what my friend, the Henredon sales representative, told me. "Never let someone else's unwillingness to do the right thing get in the way of your success, even if you have to pay for it, yourself."

Now I realized it would be up to me, and it was going to cost a lot of money to hire a professional. I knew I needed a photographer who specialized in shooting medium-to-large format images of interior, architectural settings. I also knew, like the owners of Henredon, if I did this, I could not settle for anything less than the best.

Since money was tight for me when I was nineteen years old, and I did not want to burden myself with a loan, I needed a plan to get the necessary funds.

Once I thought about it for a while, I decided to take the full commission from every third sale I made and save it for the photographer and photo sessions. Then I called some top-notch photographers and told them what I hoped to achieve.

Next, I looked through what seemed like an endless procession of portfolios. Then I chose the best photographer I could find, and asked him to quote his day rate, including a certain amount of film, custom lab work and processing. After that, I grabbed my chest and almost had a heart attack! My boss was right about the cost. However, he was wrong not to invest in these incredible sales aids.

During the next few months, I landed some impressive sales and earned what I needed to finance the photography sessions. In fact, enough money came in, by using every third commission check, to pay for a custom hand-tooled leather portfolio. I used the beautiful cover to showcase the before and after pictures of my most incredible projects.

Within the next six months, my sales were sharply increasing. I was selling 60% of the stores overall sales, and I never looked back. From that time on, I continued saving 10% of every commission check I earned to promote myself. I had made up my mind I wouldn't let anyone stand in the way of my success.

Each time I went out on appointments I took my portfolio with me. The customers enjoyed viewing the 11-inch x 14-inch photographs while I was measuring their rooms. While my portfolio kept them entertained, I drew pictures depicting what each setting would look like when the job was complete.

The custom photographs were spectacular. They added credibility to my sales pitches. This helped me land almost every project I went after. Not only did my closing ratio increase, but the size of the jobs got much larger, as well. Better yet the money I started investing in promoting myself was instrumental in helping me build my own following.

The furniture store I worked for didn't want to spend their money promoting my sales, so I used my own money to promote myself. This in turn, helped me earn my first fortune.

I could never have commanded that respect with basic snapshots, or Polaroid images, of the previous work I had preformed. My friend had taught me well! What you show a person reflects the quality and believability you will receive in return.

Most people are smart enough to understand that anyone who is willing to invest whatever it takes to show their work at its best, will probably go to extraordinary lengths to make sure your project turns out incredible too.

Salespeople usually wait for the store they work for, to invest money in advertising to promote sales. However, when the stores invest little to nothing in advertising, these salespeople suffer.

Every salesperson should learn the importance of self-promotion and budget for it accordingly. Every dollar you spend on yourself will come back to you many times over. I'm living, breathing proof of that. The investment I made in myself paid off beyond my wildest dreams.

William S. Crenshaw

CHAPTER 10

LEAD, FOLLOW, OR GET OUT OF THE WAY

The world is made up of leaders, followers and people who have not yet decided which way they want to go. But there is one thing they all have in common. It seems like everyone's mind is wired the same. From the time you are born, until the day you die, your brain is constantly searching for answers.

What will the next bright idea be? Which product will become the next best seller? Who will come up with the next winning investment strategy? When should I buy a stock, and how long should I wait to sell it? What is the best way to get out of debt, and how should I manage my money? What will the next trend in fashion be? Who can help me put an attractive wardrobe together? What hairstyle would look best on me? What color scheme should I use on my house? Which restaurant has the best food in town? Which diet plan works the best? What automobile should I

167

purchase? Who is the best mechanic in my area? What store carries the nicest furniture in town? Do you think I should do this, or do you think I should do that? Do you think I'm making the right decision? What would you do?

Every minute of every day, people ask questions about something, and every question they ask opens the door for a sale to be made. The people asking these questions look for a take-charge person who is ready, willing, and able to guide them. Are you that person?

As a salesperson, you need to understand; whoever has the most credible flow of information has the best chance to become a leader. But this does not mean that person will always be up to the task of leading. It simply means they have a tiny window of opportunity to see if they can rise to the occasion and get the job done.

If you are a leader, there is no job in the world as exciting as sales!

One of my favorite leaders from the 1960s, through the 1990s, was Lee Iacocca. Born in Allentown Pennsylvania, Lee went to Lehigh, University, in Bethlehem Pennsylvania, where he earned a degree in industrial engineering.

Then after graduating from Lehigh, he won the Wallace Memorial Fellowship and went to Princeton University where he took his electives in politics, and plastics. Following that, he then began a career at Ford Motor Company as an engineer.

Eventually, dissatisfied with that job, he switched career paths at Ford and entered the company's sales force. In sales, Lee found a new zest for life and broadened his horizons by moving up to product development. While working in that division, he is best known for being instrumental in the design of the Ford Mustang, the Lincoln Continental Mark III, and the Ford Escort. He will also be remembered for reviving the Mercury brand in the late 1960s.

Later on, Mr. Iacocca was strongly courted by the Chrysler Corporation, which was on the verge of going out of business.

After accepting a position with the Chrysler Corporation, Mr. Iacocca played a strong role in bringing about the front wheel drive Dodge Caravan, and the Plymouth Voyager Minivan. He also changed the way people thought of, and used, their family automobiles.

Mr. Iacocca obtained numerous degrees, which gave him the opportunity to aspire to lofty heights in engineering. However, he chose the field of sales and

169

marketing to pursue his passions. It was lucky for both the Ford Motor Company, and Chrysler Corporation, that he did.

When Lee got in front of an audience his leadership abilities began to shine, and there wasn't a better salesman alive to pitch a new product. The Ford Mustang was proof of that! But when the going got tough for the Chrysler Corporation, Mr. Iacocca was asked to sell an idea that would literally mean the difference between life and death for one of America's oldest and best-known companies.

In 1979, he made his greatest sales pitch of all. This speech was given to a meeting of Congress when he sold the Federal Government on the idea of guaranteeing a loan for the Chrysler Corporation.

Realizing that the company would go out of business if it did not receive a significant amount of money for a turnaround, Mr. Iacocca approached the United States Congress and asked for a loan guarantee. Not a loan, or a bailout, mind you, just a loan guarantee.

Because of the K-cars, and minivans, along with the reforms Iacocca implemented, the Chrysler Corporation quickly turned around and was able to repay the government-backed loans seven years earlier than expected.

Mr. Iacocca used his sales, and leadership capabilities, to change the course of time. Not only did he sell one dream after another to drivers all over the world, he also saved one of the largest corporations in the United States by successfully pitching an idea.

To me, that's what selling is all about. A sales pitch can be the most powerful thing on earth, but the person making the presentation has to have the ability to take charge and lead.

One of Mr. Iacocca's favorite phrases was lead, follow, or get out of the way', and if you want to become a top-notch salesperson, that says it all.

If you can lead us, get on with it, and take control of the situation. If you cannot, or you're unwilling to do so, then shut up and follow the person who can.

Most beginners entering the field of sales haven't had jobs where they were in control, so they probably haven't had the opportunity to lead. Because they were constantly taking orders from someone else, they may have become use to waiting for their boss to plot a course, and tell them what to do.

Being placed in this position usually winds up turning people into order takers and desk clerks, so they have to work hard to change old habits and begin looking ahead for things to do. These newbie's must

171

build up their courage and look for an opportunity to take charge and develop leadership skills.

Once they study the products surrounding them and open their minds to the endless possibilities that their new job in sales has to offer, these salespeople will usually find it hard to sleep at night. From this time on, they will be eager to connect with another potential client. Now that they are ready, they will have an opportunity to take charge and a mutually rewarding sale will take place.

The most valuable people in an organization are top-notch salespeople. The reason why is clear. He, or she, is usually the most knowledgeable person there when it comes to everything the company has to sell. They are also take-charge individuals who command respect for their knowledge, advice, and leadership capabilities.

Once you take charge as a salesperson, and become a leader instead of a follower, your sales will increase dramatically. You will also gain the respect of your clients and peers.

Every salesperson has the chance to lead at one time or another, but it's all up to you!

When you get an opportunity to lead a customer in the right direction always tell them what you feel is right. Never answer a customer's questions by telling then what you think they want to hear. Trying to hedge your bets with a politically correct answer can put you and your customer's relationship at risk. They need to believe that you are the one person in the world they can count on for an honest answer. When they truly believe in you, they will follow your lead. So don't blow it! Always tell it like it is.

Once you prove that you're knowledgeable, and trustworthy, your greatest challenge will come. Now the customer will leave you an opening to step up and take charge.

When this opportunity takes place, you must be ready to respond. If you follow through properly, the customer will feel assured that they are in capable hands and start relying on your judgment. This is huge when it comes to plus sales and building a lasting relationship with this individual.

Now, all of the hard work you put into studying your craft and all the daydreams you have had about that once-in-a-lifetime opportunity, have come full circle. They are right there in front of you. So, take charge and go for it!

Many of you will doubt yourself, and wonder if you have what it takes to become a leader. But it takes all kinds of people to make the world go round.

Some of our greatest leaders were incredibly smart and well-read individuals, like Thomas Jefferson. Others were inventive and quick-witted, like Benjamin Franklin. Some were incredible storytellers like Ronald Regan, and then we had visionaries like Walt Disney. But no matter what qualities other leaders had, they never out-shinned the common sense that Abraham Lincoln possessed. In him, we got the chance to see what an average person could aspire to, that was not blessed with good looks, or the finer things in life. By doing so, we realized we all have a chance to lead and succeed. If he could do it, so could we.

When you start thinking of becoming a leader in your field, don't look at yourself in the mirror and think, 'I'm so plain I can never pull this off'. If you do, just think of old Abe looking back at you saying, "Really! Surely you're not stuck with this face".

To become an extraordinary leader all you need is well-rounded knowledge about a subject, and a passion for sharing that knowledge with the people around you. You do not have to be brilliant, just sincere, and a little commonsense goes a long way.

Next, you should practice talking about your chosen subject with your friends and family. This will allow you to become comfortable in communicating your thoughts.

Then, after you finish each conversation, read more about the subject. Search for interesting, little-known tidbits of information that you can use, like seasoning, to spice up your next story. Then talk about the subject again with a different group of people.

Each time you do this, you will become more at ease with the subject, and it will eventually become second nature to you.

You should also search for any forums, or conventions, that might have speakers talking about the subject, or merchandise you intend on selling. If you get the opportunity, try to find out something new from every speaker's presentation.

If you choose to sell a manufactured product, try to arrange a meeting with the designers who created it. Then get their take on the merchandise. Sometimes you would be surprised what's in their minds.

It is also an excellent idea to probe them for their thoughts about the future of the product. Where do they see this item in the near and distant future? Do they anticipate any radical changes coming?

The more you know the better leader you can be. Remember, since we are talking about something that could be worth a lot of money to you in the near future, you should take this seriously. You want to master the subject!

Once you feel that you have truly learned everything you can about the item, or items, stand back and look at them again. This time view them from a different prospective, and try to figure out a new angle, or way to use them on your own.

I started doing this in the furniture business, when I was twenty-two years old, and I made a boatload of money manufacturing unique products that I sold in my store.

Never forget, there will always be a new way to use, and sell, an old product. And a talented salesperson will figure it out, and cash in on it before anyone else does.

When I designed and built Key West Designs in Central California, in 1969, I was on a never-ending search for new and exciting furniture and accessories for my 16,000 square foot showroom, and the two-story warehouse I used for backup merchandise.

On these buying trips, I traveled all over the United States and visited the best-known manufacturers, and most popular conventions of the day. But it wasn't in their regular showrooms that I made some of my greatest discoveries. It was often in the most unusual situations and out of the way places that I found the most valuable items to buy and sell. Those epiphanies always came about by stepping outside of the mainstream, where everyone else was shopping, and opening my mind to the new possibilities around me.

On one buying trip, I overheard the wife of a manufacturer talking to her friend about an out of the way rug merchant down by the docks. She said he had some unbelievable Persian rugs for sale at unheard of prices, and the quality was first rate.

It just so happened, the night before, I was reading a tale from, 'The Book of One Thousand and One Nights', in my hotel room. The book was about Aladdin, a street urchin who accidentally meets and falls in love with Princess Jasmine. So, the reference I overheard to Persian rugs caught my attention.

After I had finished my day's work, I took a cab to the waterfront and found the shop she had mentioned. Then I began looking around. Sure enough, the store was filled to the rafters with beautiful hand-knotted wool, and silk rugs, of every size, and color imaginable, and they were priced so low I couldn't believe my eyes.

The more I looked, the more excited I became. Then I started thinking how beautiful these exquisite rugs would look in my furniture store. At these prices, I could make four times the regular mark-up, and they would still be an excellent buy for my customers.

177

Then an incredible idea came to me! I could create a setting in one of the stores corner windows, facing Main Street, and make it look just like a scene from 'One Thousand and One Nights'. I knew it would be a real crowd pleaser!

Now my mind was filled with as many questions as thought provoking ideas. What would I do for seating arrangements, and how would I light the room? Then it dawned on me... I could use the rugs themselves to create the seats.

Just a year or so earlier, a couple of Italian designers had invented Bean Bag chairs, and they were selling like crazy! The main structure of this seating arrangement consisted of a large bag filled with Styrofoam pellets, and they were usually covered in vinyl, velvet or denim. After thinking about this, I realized I didn't have to reinvent this item. I just needed to tweak it a little.

To create my Persian rug beanbag seating arrangement, I could use a couple of 4'x6' rugs for the seat cushions and have a canvas shop make large 4'x6' bags, to sew to the bottoms. Then I could fill the bags with the same Styrofoam pellets Bean Bag chairs were filled with, and use them like a sectional in the corner of the room.

Next, for the back pillows, I could take four prayer rugs that were 2'x3' each in size, and have canvas pouches sewn to the backs of them. Once they were filled with the same Styrofoam pellets, they would make the perfect upright, back cushions. Then I could place another 6'x9' rug on the floor in front of the pillow seating arrangement, and the incredible colored patterns of the rugs would bring the setting to life.

Now all I had to do was locate the perfect brass-candlestick lighting fixtures, paintings, and accessories, throw in a gnarly wood chest, drape some fabric from the ceiling and my display would be complete.

After that, I came to an agreement with the merchant and purchased an enormous amount of rugs. Then I made a deal with a canvas shop in my hometown to manufacture the stuffed bags, and I proceeded to build my window display. We finished the set on a Friday afternoon and uncovered the windows. By the time the store had opened Saturday morning, people were already calling and coming inside to purchase our magic carpet seating arrangements. The fad continued to sell heavily for approximately three years before it slowed down. The rugs themselves never stopped selling.

This is what I'm talking about when I say... just about the time you think you've seen it all, and you

179

know everything there is to know about the items you're selling, take another look at them from a different perspective. There may be another way to use them that could make you a fortune.

You would not believe how much money my magic carpet cushions put in my bank account through the years, and that was just a small example of looking for another use of something that's right in front of you.

The same thing was true in a big way for Mr. Iacocca. He took a second look at how a conventional utility van was used. Then he observed families struggling to get their kids and other essentials in a regular car or station wagon, and a billion dollar idea lit up his mind. Not long after that the minivan was born!

One of the key elements in leadership is being willing to take the initiative to get things done. A real leader doesn't just come up with ideas. He or She thinks them through quickly and acts on them. Remember, a brilliant idea is worthless unless someone steps forward and brings it to life.

Leaders should be valued the same way. If a leader talks a great story, but never brings his or her ideas to full fruition, that leader is worthless, as well. Don't just talk... Do!

Keep your mind open and listen to what's going on around you. If you do, you'll never run out of good ideas, and you will get your chance to be a leader. Sometimes you'll lead by answering others questions and other times you'll lead by setting an example. But most often you will lead by seeing what is needed and making sure it gets done.

William S. Crenshaw

CHAPTER 11
CONNECTING THE DOTS

Some people are nearsighted, some are farsighted, and some have perfect 20-20 sight.

Some people see only what they want to see. Others see what they thought they saw, and some folks didn't see anything whatsoever.

Then there are the less fortunate people who are color blind, and the lucky ones who can see every color under the sun.

We also realize it is possible to make some people believe they are seeing what we want them to see by using the power of suggestion.

People jokingly say those who drink heavily can see pink elephants when they have had one drink too many, and some people swear they have even seen ghosts!

Then there are people who had seen the mirage of an oasis in the desert when they were dying of thirst.

183

It's even been documented that mass hysteria has been known to cause thousands of people to witness seeing the same thing, at the same time, but what they saw never actually took place at all. It was just a figment of their imagination.

But to me the scariest phenomenon of all involving sight, is watching a salesperson, or business owner, develop tunnel vision. This usually marks the beginning of their demise.

When I was in my teens and just beginning a career in the field of sales, a wise old man befriended me. He said, "Thing's around you aren't quite as they seem. You see most people have tunnel vision, and they only focus on one thing at a time.

Because they are shortsighted, and have very little imagination, they wind up spending their entire lives trying to get everything they can out of that one thing. The reality is, however, everything around us is linked together in one way or another, so you must learn to view them that way. Then connect the dots! When you finally understand what I'm talking about you will become successful, and the manner in which you do it will seem almost effortless to those around you."

As I think back about that conversation it's unbelievable how right he was, and those words changed the way I looked at everything from that day forward.

Until then, like most other people, I never stopped to think how everything I did connected to someone, or something else. It never dawned on me how each one of those connections could be turned into business opportunities, then ultimately into sales. All I was paying attention to was the business at hand, while other potential sales were hiding in plain sight.

What I failed to understand was how easy it is to preprogram your mind to the same old grind and wind up in a rut.

Because my first job in retail sales was working at a furniture store, I met people who often invited me to their homes. When I arrived at the site, however, I never paid much attention to the outside of their house, or the inside of the structure itself. My only thought was how anxious I was to see inside their living quarters. After all, the only reason I was going there was to help my customers decorate the inside of their home, and sell them beautiful furniture and accessories.

With that thought burned in my subconscious, I was oblivious to other things around me, and I continued to grind out sales like everyone else at the store.

I was literally stepping over dollars, to pick up pennies without knowing it, and I had a giant smile plastered on my face while I patted myself on the back. I thought I was really getting somewhere, and why wouldn't I feel that way? I was outselling everyone at the store, and living the good life, or so I thought!

Now, however, after that brief conversation, I could not help thinking maybe there were more opportunities out there than I had ever dreamed of.

In my case, it turned out hindsight was the clearest vision of all.

Sad to say the customers were also shorting themselves, by viewing their home using the same tunnel vision I used. It was a case of the blind leading the blind.

Customers were anxious to fix up their homes, and by entering the searching mode in their subconscious, they were ready for suggestions, but they had no idea where to begin. Since they didn't know where to start, the first thing they did was search for new furniture. Now both of us, the customer and myself, were fixated on figuring out what items would look best in their home, and neither one of us was connecting the dots to see the big picture.

In many cases, these homes were basic structures that needed detailing so they would create the perfect backdrop for the beautiful furniture and accessories.

Even the nicer houses lacked the finishing touches that would personalize each one making it different from their neighbors and friends. However, no one was thinking about that. We were all putting the cart before the horse.

What customers needed to realize was the fact that the furniture and accessories were supposed to be the finishing touch, not the cure all that would complete each home.

No matter how much furniture they purchased, their home would never look complete until each structure was trimmed-out, and finished properly. As I came to realize that, connecting the dots, and seeing the big picture started making perfect sense to me.

From that time on, I took it as a personal challenge to open each customer's mind, so each one could visualize just how incredible their homes could be with all the right details. That created a new world of possibilities for my sales career, and I had finally found a new way to utilize my art capabilities.

By learning how to see the world around me with no preset limitations, I was able to sell better than ever. It was an incredible feeling. I felt like I had unlimited possibilities, and I couldn't wait to hit the books again. I wanted to learn everything there was to know about custom building, from the ground up, including custom cabinets and trim, landscaping, masonry, swimming pools, and water features.

Once I learned everything I could about all of these elements, I was able to utilize any or all of them in my projects, and map out a perfect plan. This gave me the opportunity to create a total environment, inside and out, and my customers loved it! Now I had come full circle as a salesperson and designer.

Looking back when I first began my new job in sales I had an open mind, and looked for every piece of information I could find on furniture and accessories. Then I started using my newfound knowledge to help me move merchandise. Before long, all I could think of was selling more furniture. Sadly, by this time, tunnel vision had already taken over my subconscious.

The scariest thing of all about tunnel vision is the fact that most people who have it, don't even know they do. Just like a diabetic, they can't feel it, or see it, so how could they realize that this thought-draining disease has already totally taken over their mind.

Tunnel vision is probably, by far, the single greatest threat to a salesperson's career. This loss of peripheral vision can potentially blind them, and keep them from seeing their full potential.

Tunnel vision is also the cause for almost every other business in the world to shrivel up, and die a slow death. This phenomenon is sad to see, and it usually takes place when a vibrant business locks into a certain trend, or sales pattern, and doesn't see the times around them changing. Because of their tunnel vision, and unwillingness to change, the storeowners' once-vibrant business can wind up falling by the wayside.

Any business owner who develops tunnel vision can be successful today and wind up broke tomorrow.

What most newbie's in business fail to understand is the fact that almost everything in their store has a certain shelf life including their merchandise, backdrops and displays, as well. That means they have to avoid developing tunnel vision, and keep their eyes open for the next hot idea that will catch the public's attention, and keep their sales alive.

That next shift in customer preferences can come in the form of colors, styles, patterns, sounds, textures, smells, or new fads of the time, and you better be able to pick up on the new movement as it flows into the mainstream. If you can't, you better surround yourself with the talented people who can!

Never stop looking deeply into everything around you, and make it a game to connect the dots. You should always be asking, what if.

It is equally important for a store's sales staff to keep their look alive, and connected to the times. If the salespeople start to look old and funky, that form of tunnel vision can mean their days are limited, and their sales numbers can begin to fall off.

Every salesperson must remember their customers are constantly changing too. Not only are your long time customers moving steadily ahead, keeping up with the times, but their children are, as well!

When you first start your career in sales, you're so busy trying to learn what you're doing, that you can lose track of time. This is when tunnel vision starts sneaking up on you!

In the beginning, every satisfied customer you add to your list will give you a false feeling of security, making you believe your future is safe. Your real future, however, rests in the hands of their children. They will be the new customers in your future, so you will need to learn how to court them. To do that, you must keep up with the changing times!

The personal style you used in the beginning of your career won't seem too cool to your customers in the future, so don't become outdated. Every so often shift gears and pick up on a new look. This will let your customers see that you aren't developing tunnel vision. You're in tune with the times, and still the perfect go-to person.

Whether you are a salesperson, or a buyer, you have to keep your mind open for new ways to connect the dots. Your future depends on it!

The business world is constantly evolving, and there are new opportunities for sales popping up every day, and in every kind of business. Many of the hottest new items you will have a chance to cash in on in the future will actually come from an industry that skirts your own. Because it's not actually something that's part of your field, you might have a tendency to overlook it. When you are in sales, however, being able to spot these items, or trends, will mean the difference between whether you're thought of as the best at what you do, or just another wannabe.

When I see children look at something new for the first time, I see the wonder in their eyes, and I can't help thinking that's the way every adult salesperson and buyer, should approach their jobs at the work place.

Once I had proven myself as a top-notch salesperson, my boss invited me to tag along on a buying trip. This sounded like fun to me, but I had no idea how educational the trip would be.

Buying merchandise took the selling approach that I had become use to, and literally flipped it upside down. Here, once again, a smart buyer had to learn how to see the big picture and connect the dots, but from a very different prospective.

If a buyer purchased something simply because he or she liked it, and based their decision on that alone they might be stuck with that item for a long time and have to mark it down to get rid of it. Because of that, they had to learn to leave their own personal likes, and dislikes, out of the equation when it came to buying.

After I went on a few of these buying trips my boss said, "I think you're ready to try buying on your own, but there are a few things I want you to remember. First, you want to keep your mind on your customers. You've watched customers in our store, listened to their conversations, and sold them thousands of dollars worth of merchandise. Now you have a better than average feeling as to what they would like in their homes. You also have an idea what they might be willing to spend for those items. So play it safe in the beginning, and don't take chances with your first budget." He then went on to say, "When you see an item that you think would be perfect for the store, don't rush up and turn the price tag over until you've determined what you can sell it for. Once you have a retail price fixed firmly in your mind, then it's time to find out what the wholesale price is. If the price you think you can sell the item for, including freight, is equal to one-half of the cost or less, then buy it. If the item costs more, walk away and don't look back. Never talk yourself into purchasing an item if you will have to ask more for it than you originally thought you could get. Most important of all... don't fall in love with your merchandise, unless you intend on taking it home with you."

This time, working as a buyer instead of seller, I would have to connect the dots by instinctively figuring out what items the public would purchase, and just how much they would be willing to spend for them.

Now, my sales experience would prove to be more valuable than ever before. If my decisions were right, the store and all the salespeople working there could have an incredible year. Everyone could benefit from my intuition. But it would be disastrous if I were wrong.

They say you never really understand another person's situation until you walk a mile in their shoes. Now I was beginning to understand what went on in the mind of a buyer. It was fascinating how many different things had to be taken into consideration before a buyer purchased merchandise for a store. And the art of merchandising a showroom, and buying back up merchandise for the warehouse, was another task all together.

I never seriously thought about it before, but a great buyer has to be a top-notch salesperson too. Each one just represents the flip side of the other.

Now, I saw our store and warehouse differently than I had before, and I couldn't stop thinking of all the beautiful items our customers would be interested in for their homes and businesses.

One of the most interesting things of all, however, was learning how to stay at least one-step ahead of your competition. You see, every storeowner within a hundred mile radius of one another tries their best to discover what the other stores in their area are carrying. Then they try to knock them off by undercutting their prices. So we use to shop the major markets in our area first, just to see what they were buying. Then we would purchase a railcar load of the best-looking merchandise they had chosen to use peppered throughout our store, and we would short mark it at cost plus 10%. We would always display this reduced price on a regular price tag, so it would show no sign of a markdown.

Then we would go thousands of miles away to another market to search for unique merchandise and ship it in to fill our store. Next, we would code this inventory, so the other stores couldn't shop us and discover whom the manufacturers were. After that, we would use a regular mark up on these items.

Once we displayed everything in our showroom it was comical watching the customers. They would spot an item that they had looked at in a competitors store, then ask is that piece on sale. Our answer would always be... no, that's our regular price on that item. Is there anything else I can answer for you? Before you knew it, everyone in town was talking about how reasonable our prices were, and our competitors looked like pirates.

This was all part of the selling game, and it kept everyone on their toes.

Once a new fad had come on the scene, and everyone had made purchases, the markets would usually cool down for a few months. During those markets, you would hear the major buyers complaining about how the market was slow, and there wasn't anything new to look at, but the best buyers never ran out of interesting things to see. We were fascinated with everything!

There were always new materials to look at and unique displays around every corner. Just when the other buyers thought that they had seen it all, there was a mind-blowing lighting effect used to set off a display that would catch my attention. I knew my customers would be drawn in by this exciting new effect, and it would help me sell more merchandise in a poorly lit corner of my store. That one find alone could make the buying trip worthwhile.

Once again, tunnel vision was taking its toll, but, not on me.

Most buyers at the market looked for merchandise that had a different appearance from the time before. But the new five-year-fad had already been introduced to the public a few months earlier. Now, that same look would be everywhere you went for at least four more years.

For anyone with tunnel vision that meant that there was nothing new to look at during the market. However, to buyers who weren't afflicted with that disease, every new merchandise mart was an eye-opener, filled to the brim with new things to see, and exciting ways to set up displays in your store. What's more, the accessory vendors were always coming up with new goodies that offered the retailers exciting opportunities to pump up their sales volume and increase their markup. All these people had to do was open their eyes and take a second look around. Then connect the dots!

After 53 years of buying and selling every kind of merchandise, you can think of, I still get excited when I look around at the opportunities that exist.

That is why I say, when it comes to sales, there's a job for everyone. If the job market looks tight and you don't see any openings when you first go out looking for work, then open your eyes a little wider and go out looking again.

William S. Crenshaw

CHAPTER 12
A MONEY MAKING MACHINE

Have you ever noticed how different a person's demeanor is when they've connected with their talents, compared to someone who hasn't found their groove yet in life? That air of confidence and self-assuredness is one of the main ingredients found in a successful salesperson's bag of tricks.

A noticeable difference between the wealthiest salespeople and all the rest, is how diversified their talents are, and how many different ways they use those talents in their sales efforts.

This phenomenon is made even more fascinating by the fact that any talent will do!

A few exceptional salespeople are gifted storytellers, while others are incredible debaters. Many of our best salespeople are artists or musicians. Then there are those who are talented athletes and fishermen. We also have inspiring salespeople who design and build everything imaginable, and there are those who are masters of trivial pursuit. Other top salespeople are unbelievable mechanics, seamstresses, cooks, and wine coinsures. Some well-read salespeople are brilliant historians, and there are those who love to grow things. Many of the best salespeople I've met love to listen to good music and go to the movies. Then there are those who enjoy teaching and enlightening others. There are also top-notch salespeople who are wizards when it comes to financial matters and salesmen and women who love showing off in the latest fashions. All in all, there is a multitude of different talents and interests shared by top-notch salespeople all over the world. And each person will utilize them in their own unique way.

Most successful salespeople think of themselves as walking-talking-mobile-stores, and they have something to offer everyone.

The best-of-the-best in sales, however, have learned to connect every one of their personal talents, and interests, to their sales efforts. By intertwining their talents with their sales efforts, they're connecting all the dots and reaping the rewards.

Almost without exception, the richest people in sales bring in monthly paychecks from more than one source. As long as the different businesses they are selling for are noncompetitive with each other, there's no conflict of interest. In some cases, one sale will actually instigate a sale with another complementary company, making it a win-win situation for everyone concerned. This type of sale usually winds up bringing in commission checks from two or more companies for the salesperson who pitched the sale.

The only exceptions to this rule are the most highly sought after sales representatives who are paid huge sums of money to represent one, and only one product, or company. These sales reps usually bring in not only large monthly commission checks, but also substantial year-end bonuses for their unique sales abilities.

When I worked in the furniture business, and learned how to connect the dots, I discovered a way to use my art talents to help customers visualize what their homes could look like before they invested any money in buying furniture. By utilizing my art pad like a crystal ball, there was no need for the trial and error approach everyone else was using. Once I started illustrating inside views of my customer's homes, my furniture sales shot up dramatically.

Next, I began drawing pictures of built-in-bookcases, exotic doors, ceilings, and interior trim behind the furniture, and lo and behold, these same customers couldn't wait to purchase those items too!

Then I created renderings with open windows to the background, so I could draw in a beautiful swimming pool and landscape behind the furniture, and my customers wound up hiring me to help them build those items, as well!

Now I had commission checks coming in from all over town and I was just getting started. It wasn't long before I was able move into a beautiful home filled with gorgeous furniture, and pay cash for a shiny new sports car.

All of this good fortune came my way because I didn't walk away from my other talents when I chose a career in sales, far from it! I found a new way to use my art abilities to enhance my sales instead of giving up on a career in commercial art. Now, at a young age, I had discovered one of the best-kept secrets of getting rich in sales. You've got to use every skill you possess, and put all of your interests into play in every sale you make. If you've got it, flaunt it!

When I looked back, that was what my friend the car salesman had done, and it worked for him. He connected his love of customizing automobiles with his customer's desires to have their brand-new cars in their favorite colors, along with custom leather upholstery and shinny chrome rims. He realized there were many rich people in his sales area, and they wanted what they wanted, when they wanted it, no matter what the cost. Because he connected the dots and used his talent to bring their dreams to reality, he became the richest car salesman in Central California.

Time after time, throughout my career in sales, I watched as one salesperson after another wove their special talents, and interests, into their sales efforts. The most successful ones always had an angle, and it always paid off big time in their bank accounts.

One tall, handsome salesman, who worked at my furniture store in the early 1970s, loved beautiful clothing, and he was always dressed to the nines. When he wasn't at the furniture store, you could usually find him at one of the nicest clothing shops in the area. While he was there, he would check out the latest arrivals in new fashion, and spend most of his commission checks on clothes.

Since he was a gifted interior designer, he had a natural ability to create beautiful clothing ensembles by mixing and matching colors and textures. Because he had such great admiration for the fashion industry in general, he had taken the time to learn the proper way to build the perfect wardrobe for both formal and informal occasions, and his skills didn't go unnoticed.

Almost every week one of his customers would ask him to help them pick out something special for an event they would be attending, or a trip they were preparing for, and rumors of his good taste spread fast. Since these requests usually came from his customer's, he always felt obligated to meet them at one of his favorite clothing stores. There, he would help them choose the perfect combination of clothing and accessories. Before long, the owners of these stores came to realize how valuable his talents were, and on more than one occasion, they asked him if he would ever consider coming to work for them, but he always graciously said no.

Then one day, he told the owner of the nicest shop in the area that he had a proposition for him. He said, "I have the ability to sell a lot of clothing for you, both in your store, and on location in the custom home's I decorate. As you have previously seen, people ask for my advice, and they shop in the stores I recommend. What if I went to work for you as an outside salesman, that would give us both the chance to have our cake and eat it too! I could continue to work in my chosen trade as an interior designer, and sell clothing for you on the side." Then he said, "If you like the idea, this is how I wish to be compensated for my efforts. First, I would expect you to furnish me with free samples of your newest clothing, which I will use to model on a daily basis at the design studio where I work. Second, I would expect a commission for every sale I make, and third, I would need to bring clients in after regular hours to help them build their wardrobes. What do you say? Do we have a deal?"

The storeowner was dumbfounded! Then he shook his head and said, "Yes, it's a deal."

Later on that day, my designer came to me and shared the story of what had just happened, hoping I would be ok with his bold move. I was thrilled for him! Now he was able to see his dreams come true, and he didn't have to choose between the two professions. They were a perfect fit for both of us.

Within six months, he nearly doubled his income by utilizing both of his talents, and because he was able to get his clothing free, it seemed as though he was making even more than that.

Four years after that, he was offered a partnership in a new high-end clothing store where he received a 40% interest for his buying skills, display techniques, and outside sales capabilities. He was able to achieve that, and keep his job as an interior designer, by utilizing all of his talents and not giving up any of his dreams. He had the courage and determination to go for it!

As for me, I had the happiest and best-dressed interior designer in town, and his sales kept growing. I learned that happy sales people generate the most business, so I never tried to hold a salesperson down.

Early on in my sales career, I witnessed the same thing take place when a lady who had worked with me, started handing out free samples of her cooking to customers. This lady loved to create mouthwatering treats, and she used them as gifts to say thank you to her customers.

Before beginning her career in sales, she was a dedicated housewife who loved to cook. And her husband was a California Highway Patrolman. To her, their life was a dream world, but it soon came crashing down when he was involved in a high-speed chase that put him in the hospital. That left her the main breadwinner in the family, and she had no work experience whatsoever outside of her home.

What she did have, however, was a marvelous personality, a way with putting furniture together, and a knack for making your taste buds tingle. She also knew how to keep everyone talking about her!

I remember her first year in sales, and how desperate she was for income, but because she had been using all of her talents, things were about to change for the better.

When her husband was finally able to return to work, she decided to throw him a big surprise party, and she invited everyone she knew, including her business associates, and customers from work. This time she pulled out all the stops, and laid out a feast the likes of which I had never seen before. What made the affair even more interesting was the fact that her sister was just as talented in the kitchen as she was, and their food was to die for. With her design skill's, she was able to create a memorable setting for the party, and all the guests, including her husband, had the time of their lives.

The following week at work, everyone was still talking about the incredible evening, and all that wonderful food. Then it happened! The first call came in asking her if she would host, and cater, a large party for a wealthy rancher. Then another call came in, and another. Before long, her services were booked weeks in advance, and her sister, and both of their husbands joined in on the activities.

What began as a passion for cooking had now turned into a booming catering business and she was picking up momentum as a top-notch salesperson at the furniture store. As it turned out both activities, decorating people's homes, and the catering-business, fit together perfectly and her financial worries were over for good!

In the years that followed, she became a professional member of the Interior Design Society, and turned out to be a top-producing saleswoman.

As for the catering operation, it blossomed into an incredible full-blown party destination located in a refurbished barn. The barn was on a walnut ranch just outside town, and they purchased it with the profits from the business.

Through the years, I've come to realize that everyone has a hidden talent. Sadly, most of them are set aside because the person who possesses the talent winds up taking a steady job that goes in a different direction from their dreams.

Some people put their talent aside to do what they think is right for their family, and trudge on through life doing something that brings them little to no satisfaction at all. Surprisingly, however, abandoning your talent, and dreams, can wind up achieving the exact opposite of what you wished for. You see, everyone around you benefits from your dreams, and hidden talents. Not just you!

When you are dreaming out loud, and working to improve your talents, your wife, or husband, children, and friends, all gain something from that experience.

The hope, determination, and hard work, you invest in pursuing your talent, will fortify their courage. Your efforts as a role model make it proof positive that their dreams are worth chasing. Dreams really can come true! By at least trying to succeed, you've already become a winner in their eyes.

Even, if you find it necessary to take a job doing something entirely different from what you originally dreamed of, you can still find a way to keep your dreams alive by working them into your surroundings. By getting involved in sales, you will open yourself up to unimaginable opportunities to use your talents like never before.

Most people don't realize it, but their unused talents are like hidden treasures, however, no one will discover them unless you bring them to the surface.

The field of sales is undoubtedly the most diversified career in existence, and it opens the door to creativity, but you have to open your eyes and see the trees in the forest. If you're not paying attention to what's going on all around you, everything you're looking at can blend in together, and it might seem like you have come to a dead end.

When you notice everyone else with a puzzled look on their face, and hear the voice of doubt coming from their lips, opportunity is knocking. So for goodness sake, when that happens, open the door to your mind, and let the inspiration in. Now it's time to use your talent, and creativity, to move forward and make something happen.

A gifted salesperson can take the ordinary and turn it into something extraordinary. Think how important that can be in someone's life! Not only is that ability helpful when it comes to moving merchandise, it's also invaluable when it comes to motivating, and inspiring the people around you.

I've seen workers stay late, without pay, to get a job done because they were motivated to do so by an exceptional salesperson. I've also watched a graphic artist throw a week's work away, and burn the midnight-oil rebuilding a project, to try and live up to the quality that his client represents. He went to all that effort just because the client had inspired him.

Situations like this happen every day because people use their talent to inspire others. Now, they reach down deep inside and try a little harder to be better than what the average person might be.

There are so many different ways that people use sales in their everyday lives it boggles the mind. That's why I truly believe that the field of sales offers a job opportunity for everyone, including you! You just have to think about what you enjoy surrounding yourself with, and start leaning in that direction. Once you fit in those surroundings, look for different ways you can weave your talents into your sales efforts, and start reaping the rewards.

One of the most interesting cases of someone using their talents in a roundabout way, through sales, to achieve an insurmountable goal, happened when GE hired Ronald Regan to work as their spokesperson, and ambassador.

From September 26, 1954, until 1962, Ronald Reagan worked as the host of the General Electric Theater on TV and toured the United States as GE's spokesperson.

Throughout that eight-year period, he visited approximately 135 of GE's research and manufacturing facilities in over 30 states and delivered as many as 14 speeches a day. During those factory visits, Reagan met with approximately 250,000 blue-collar workers, and mid-management personnel, where he took questions, and sold the company's concept of unity to all of GE's employees.

That eight-year sales tour gave Reagan an opportunity to practice speaking and answer questions to sympathetic, but demanding, audiences. During that time, he was able to polish his speeches and

211

incorporate the events of the day into every talk he gave.

That experience and GE's employees served as a widespread focus group while Ronald Reagan molded his vision of America. It was also that period of time, when he shaped his political opinions, nurtured his ambitions, and perfected his negotiating skills.

Just imagine what a unique set of circumstances the union between GE, and Ronald Reagan was.

General Electric needed the services of a gifted salesperson, and communicator, to help them bridge the gap between their employees, and their sprawling empire, and the movie studios had recently dropped Ronald Regan. So the timing was perfect. Theirs was a match made in heaven!

This was a terrific opportunity, so Reagan took the sales position. Once he began the tour for General Electric, he used his charisma, and talent as a gifted speaker, to reach out to thousands of people. While he was fulfilling his duties for GE he also had the perfect opportunity to inject his thoughts on political matters of the day, and GE furnished him with the perfect audience. Eventually those speeches would propel Reagan into the most powerful position in America by helping him become the 40th President of the United States.

Looking back, I'm sure President Reagan never thought he would become a salesperson for GE, especially when he was holding a beautiful actress in his arms on the set of a major motion picture in Hollywood. However, in 1954, he became one.

I am also certain he never thought he would become America's 40th President when he signed on as a salesperson for GE, but that also happened.

In fact, you would be safe in betting President Reagan never actually knew what the future held in store for him, but he proved anything is possible!

All the people I've written about have proven beyond a shadow of a doubt, that the future just might have something spectacular in store for me. So I use my talents every chance I get, and so far they've taken me on the adventure of a lifetime!

William S. Crenshaw

CHAPTER 13
DON'T BECOME COMPLACENT

Looking back at my first five years in sales it's amazing how well I did. All I really knew about selling back then was... you had to work hard, never worry about what time it was, learn everything there is to know about the products you are selling, and utilize all of the talents that the good Lord has given you.

Amazingly, that had been enough to help me earn my first fortune, but that seemed to be as far as I could go without learning some new tricks.

For the first few years, after my partner and I opened Key West Designs, the business never stopped growing. Key West was the most exciting new furniture store to open in Central California in the 1970s, and we thought the hype would never end. There were new customers visiting the store every day, and people couldn't stop talking about the fantastic new design studio.

215

With a constant flow of activity and enthusiastic customers singing our praises, word-of-mouth alone kept our profits increasing each year!

As for advertising, we ran two closeout sales annually during market times, and that was all we had to do to keep the wheels greased and the money flowing.

Back then, everyone was patting us on the back, and we couldn't help feeling proud of ourselves, but that was about to change.

As we moved into our fourth year of doing business the store's momentum started to taper off, and our profits reached a plateau. It felt like the shine was beginning to wear off the new image we had worked so hard to build, and our customers seemed almost bored with our selling efforts.

Now my partner and I had our first serious discussion since the store opened, and you could feel the tension in the air.

For the next few months, no matter how hard we worked, or what new angles we tried, we couldn't seem to generate new interest in our operation. Even running a sale here and there didn't change things much. It seemed like we were on a merry-go-round, stuck in one place, and we were going nowhere fast. At that time, I realized we would need to do something, and do it soon, or we might start sliding backwards. It seemed like the only way we could drastically increase our sales would be to start a full-blown advertising campaign, but it would have to be unique to achieve our goals.

If we reached out to a larger audience, and advertised the store in a new light, I was sure we could increase our sales and our net profits, as well. I also believed that if we approached our old and new customers in just the right way, we wouldn't have to offer discounted-prices to bring them into the store.

Giving things away, or playing let's make a deal, seemed to be what the other stores did when they were going through hard times, or had run out of new ideas. We were not down-and-out; we just needed to jump-start our beautiful business to get going in the right direction again.

What made things even scarier was the fact that we had started trying to bring in business the same way everyone else was (with sales), and that was totally wrong!

Our success during the first three years came from being a leader, not a follower, so it was time to take charge again, and set a new pace going in a different direction.

217

One valuable lesson I learned, as a child is you cannot buy good friends. The same is true in business. Whether you are a storeowner, or a salesperson, you can't buy loyal customers with discounted prices and gimmicks. You have to earn them!

A few months earlier, before my partner and I had this discussion, I had gone out and about on one of my field trips to check on all the other stores in the area. I wanted to see how they looked, and what kind of activity they were generating. After making the rounds everyone's business seemed as slow as mine, and I came back from my outing just as confused as I was before I left.

Now, six months later, the slowdown was starting to worry me, so I met with my partner and talked to him about my concerns. To give him a feeling of just how slow things were all around us, I decided to take him on an outing, so he could witness the lull first hand.

Once we looked through some of the same retail store's I had visited a few months earlier, it hit me like a ton of bricks!

Nothing had changed... not one thing had changed in any of the store's I looked through before, and nothing had changed during that same period in our own showroom either! That was the reason everything had come to a standstill! We had stopped flirting with our customers, and the romance was gone. All of us were guilty of boring our customers to death. No wonder they had stopped coming into our stores, they had already seen it all!

As storeowners, we had become so full of ourselves, and complacent, that we started taking our customers for granted. Complacency is the number one cause of breakups in any relationship, and we had never taken that into consideration as a reason for our business slowing down. We thought the same customers would keep coming back to our store, time after time, and bring their friends, because it was the best-looking place in town. What we had all neglected to realize, however, was the fact that once our customer's had memorized what we had to offer, and realized nothing was going to change, there was no reason to return.

Now I understood what we had to do to resurrect the excitement at our furniture store, and bring our customers back again. I knew we could turn things around, and keep the momentum going, if we rolled up our sleeves, dug-in, and changed our displays on a regular basis. To achieve this, I decided to redecorate every vignette in the store at least once every other month. That was a tall order considering the fact that our fully vignetted showroom covered 16,000 square feet.

In order to create the illusion that everything in the store was new and different each time a customer returned, I decided never to use any two items together again in the same setting. Then, just to keep our customers off balance I would bring new merchandise down from the warehouse and rotate it with our floor stock on regular intervals. Since our entire store was built around an eclectic style of design, the collector look would fit us well. By continually shuffling all of our furniture and accessories, and reinventing our total look every sixty days, I knew that I would be able to keep our customers guessing, and blow their minds.

Now, in order to achieve all this, and build the perfect advertising campaign, my partner and I also realized we would either have to locate an awesome advertising company, and work with them side-by-side to get the look and feel we were after, or we would have to create the ads ourselves.

To me, the answer to this dilemma was simple. I had dreamed of becoming a commercial artist as far back as I could remember, so this was destiny knocking on my door. It was time for me to kill two birds with one stone and open my own advertising agency. That year, in 1975, I opened Sutter Creek Advertising,

Inc. in the back, of our 16,000 square foot furniture store, 'Key West Designs, and I embarked on building my first full-blown advertising campaign.

In order to surprise the public with this concept and keep the overall theme of the stores continuous, new look flowing harmoniously with the advertising campaign, we began by building the ads first. Then we redecorated the inside of the showroom.

During this period, I also chose a hook-line for our ads, and the phrase read... **Always Something New At Key West Designs!**

Since our furniture store was a retail operation, I needed to utilize all the mass media my new advertising budget could afford, and I based my budget on a percentage of our gross sales.

Next, I needed to determine which audience was more likely to respond to my advertising campaign and what radio and TV stations they would listen to. Then I decided what times, of the day or night I could catch this audience watching certain programs, and how many times a week I would air our ads.

After that, I figured out what parts of the newspaper's and magazines my new customers would be most likely to make eye contact with, to spot my store's ads. Then I determined how large each ad should be to create the most impact, without wasting

221

money by over-sizing an ad when it wasn't necessary to do so.

Last, but not least, I sampled every radio station, television station, newspaper and magazine that reached out to my new, potential customers. I did this, in order to determine what genres this diversified group of people would be most likely to listen to, watch, or read.

Now I had determined where I wanted to place our ads, and how many ads I could afford to run. I had also chosen the drive times for radio and TV ads, along with the scale of the print ads I would be placing. All that remained then was to approach each group of people who I wished to lure into our store in a manner that tastefully appealed to them, and that was a worthy challenge!

Since Central California consists of farmers, dairymen, manufacturers, builders, bankers, doctors, dentists, lawyers, teachers, preachers, accountants, shopkeepers, hair stylists, architects, business people, truckers, mechanics, and every nationality under the sun, this wasn't going to be easy.

Then I remembered, sometimes the easiest way to figure out what to do in a tough situation is watch what everyone else is doing, and then do the exact opposite. That step will usually take you in the right direction.

To utilize that approach I took a week and started studying different radio stations to find out what other stores ads sounded like. Sure enough, almost instantly one ad after another seemed to jump out at me, and scream what were you thinking of when you placed that ad on this station!

I heard country style ads on soft jazz stations, and polished debonair ads on country stations, and both of those styles were playing between rock-and-roll hits. When I stopped and paid attention to each ad, it was unreal how lost everyone seemed to be. There was no harmony between the music you were listening to, and the ads placed on any station.

I was also surprised how silly some ads were. Then others were downright nerve racking, or annoying. If these advertisements were placed to chase away customers, the companies who ran them were succeeding!

Before this, I had just tuned out annoying ads in my mind, or turned down the radio, and I didn't think anymore about them. Now, however, I could clearly see what a giant mistake these advertisers had made. There was no quick fix when it came to building the perfect advertising campaign. You could not simply build one ad and place it on every station without making a fool of yourself, and wasting your advertising dollars. In order to be successful, I needed to create a series of different commercials for each audience I wanted to approach. Only then would each ad have a chance to reach my intended listener, and be appreciated for what it was. It was also going to be important to entertain the audience with the ads I created. Then they would listen when my ads came on, instead of turning them down, or mentally tuning them out. To achieve this, I decided to go after four groups of listeners.

First, I created a series of ads tailored specifically for the smooth jazz clientele. These customers were predominately: white-collar workers, doctors, lawyers, accountants, architects, bankers, teachers, business, and professional people.

Next, I built a collection of ads that warmed up to country music listeners. This group of customers was predominately blue-collar and included farmers, truckers, dairymen, and tradespeople of all kinds.

After that, I created a series of ads that reached out and touched everyone who grew up listening to rock and roll music. I used those ads to bridge the gap between the twenty and thirty year old listeners.

Then finally, I enlisted the aid of a young senior in high school to help me prepare a collection of ads that would appeal to the youngest people on my list. These kids were commonly overlooked by businesses that thought they were of no value, but I realized they would be my next budding crop of customers in the not so distant future.

I now had the perfect ad to run on each station, and I could communicate with the audience in a manner that would satisfy them instead of turning them off. What made this approach even better was the fact that I could please crossover listeners, as well.

As I began building newspaper, and magazine ads, I chose a theme that tied Key West to a never-ending search for beautiful and unique treasures from around the world. Our store was the final destination for all of these incredible objects, and we would use the ads as invitations to invite everyone to come to our showroom and discover what had just arrived.

Next, I started building our television commercials to play up the idea that there was always something new at Key West Designs.

Our logo featured an illustrated castle, which was placed in a cameo to the left, and a quaint cottage with a white picket fence, in a cameo to the right. The two cameos were connected by a banner that read, "We will decorate your castle, or your cottage." It conveyed the message that we had something for everyone. No job was too large or small for Key West Designs. By playing up the unique beauty of our store, and the one-of-a-kind merchandise we were bringing in from all over the world, we could attract new customers throughout California. All we had to do was, keep our store looking new and fresh, and tease potential customers with this alluring advertising campaign to get them into our showroom.

Now it was time to prepare our showroom for the public. To begin our new adventure, I walled-in a room just off the loading dock at the back of our store, and created a staging area that was hidden from the public's view. This room opened to an elevator that went straight up to our two-story warehouse, and it was equal in size to our largest vignette. Then I chose a night crew to help me rearrange the showroom after hours.

To start things off we began by totally stripping one set at a time. Then we vacuumed, dusted, and polished everything thoroughly before we started building a new set.

I had purposely designed the walls and backdrops in the showroom using unique, earthy textures of wood, stone, and wallpaper, to make every piece of furniture and accessory stand out prominently. The deep neutral colors of these backdrops allowed me to change color schemes, and styles, without any trouble at all, and perfect lighting effects did the rest.

When the last display was complete, we began running the new advertising campaign. That approach paid off beyond our wildest expectations!

As the first flow of foot-traffic started to arrive, which mainly consisted of our previous customers, the excitement began to unfold again. This time each customer seemed surprised that everything looked different. Then the fun really began! Next, those customers came back a few weeks later and brought a friend. After that, many of the same people returned to look at something they were interested in, only to find out it was gone. And the race was on.

Our sales started taking off again! Customers, who had previously looked at an item nonchalantly then went home to think about it, wouldn't take that chance anymore. Now when they saw something that they liked they would have a salesperson tag it on the spot. They were nervous someone else might snatch it out from underneath them. You see every time a customer came in; nothing was the same. Customers thought that our merchandise was selling so fast they had to make up their minds immediately, or the item would be gone.

It was unbelievable what a difference this new strategy and a proper advertising campaign had made. That year our sales doubled, and we never got complacent again. We also became real believers in the power of advertising.

Over the next three years, our furniture stores business kept growing and so did my advertising agency. In fact, the advertising agencies business began to diversify from retail customers to building, manufacturing, transportation, agriculture, and service businesses of all kinds, and the field of sales began to take on a completely new appeal for me.

Until now, I had no idea how diversified the sales field was. Retail sales, on Main Street, actually played the smallest part of the over-all-sales-game, and that intrigued me. Once you ventured off Main Street, and headed out of town, it was unbelievable how many different things there were to sell.

By this time, I also had a better understanding how important advertising was. However, I had just scratched the surface when it came to learning how to use this vital new source to build sales.

As it turned out, every type of business experienced slow downs, and trend changes, exactly like what I had gone through at my store and most of them didn't have a clue how to overcome that phenomenon.

Sadly, most companies thought all they needed to prosper was to build an exemplary business, and good word-of-mouth would take care of everything else. I knew from experience that wasn't so. When you're out of sight, you're out of mind, and good word-of-mouth ceases to exist. I was also surprised to find out that most storeowners just sat by the phone waiting for sales to pick up when business was slow. I realized that's just plain nuts! When a business is starving it has to be fed, or it starts to die a slow and painful death. It's unbelievable how much money a business can lose waiting for its sales to turn around on its own.

Albert Einstein once said, "The definition of insanity is to do the same thing over and over, each time hoping for a different result". I had learned from experience, the best way to turn a slow business around is to change what you are doing, and aggressively advertise. To be successful in business and keep growing you have to be willing to invest in your property, equipment and inventory, as well as the advertising materials it takes to keep your customers thinking and talking about you.

William S. Crenshaw

If you would like to read more about how I've used all of my talents in sales to make my dreams come true, purchase my autobiography titled, <u>PURE MAGIC,</u> A little-known formula for success. I think you'll find the formula interesting, and the journey entertaining, as well.

William S. Crenshaw

ABOUT THE AUTHOR

Before Bill became an author he spent forty-six years honing his sales skills in the design, corporate and entrepreneurial worlds. For eleven years he was an interior designer and co-founded a sixteen thousand square foot design studio in Central California, Key West Designs. During that time, Bill took the art of retail sales to a whole new level.

In 1975 he opened an advertising agency named Sutter Creek Advertising, Incorporated. There he pursued his life-long ambition of becoming a commercial artist, and got his first taste of outside sales.

In 1985, a banker discovered Bill's unique talent of creating memorable advertising campaigns using his original form of Pop art. He then commissioned Bill to create a keepsake souvenir poster for sale to the masses.

Within three years Bill's poster art had sold in the millions, and three of his posters were hanging in the White House.

Today, you'll find Bill hard at work writing his newest collection of books about the wonderful world of sales.

To find out what's new with Bill contact him at:mailto:billcrenshaw47@yahoo.com

William S. Crenshaw